Elementary Forestry

B. McManus Collins
Fred M. White

 Reston Publishing Company, Inc., Reston, Virginia
A Prentice-Hall Company

Library of Congress Cataloging in Publication Data

Collins, B. McManus.
    Elementary forestry.

    Bibliography: p.
    Includes index.
    1. Forests and forestry.   2. Forests and
forestry—United States.   I. White, Fred M.
II. Title.
SD373.C62   634.9   81-1739
ISBN 0-8359-1647-2   AACR2

10 9 8 7 6 5 4 3 2 1

Printed in the United States of America

In memory of

Dr. Sherwood Githens, Jr.
Former Professor of Science Education, Emeritus
Duke University

He was tireless in the pursuit of excellence in
education, and the sine qua non of this textbook

Contents

Preface

Elementary Forestry was written to acquaint its readers with the development and the current status of forestry in the United States and elsewhere in the world, and to predict possible developments in forestry and forest products that may take place in the future. It is intended to be primarily informative and only semi-technical. It is hoped that the readers of this book will have a greater understanding of the diversity of technology and science embraced by modern forestry, and a greater appreciation of the importance of forests and forestry; and that as a result, some of its readers will discover a professional field in which they can work with maximum satisfaction and happiness in life.

The authors were aided during the composition of the text with information, illustrations, and contructive criticism by a number of forestry people, including Drs. Louis Metz and Carol Wells of the Forestry Sciences Laboratory (USDA—Forestry Service) in the Research Triangle Park, N.C.; Dr. Donald Steensen; N.C. State University School of Forestry; Dr. George Duthrow, U.S. Forestry Service; and Dr. Thomas G. Wilkinson of the Durham Southern High School faculty. Photographs were made available by the U.S. Forestry Service, the U.S. Soil Conservation Service, the N.C. Department of Conservation & Natural Resources; the N.C. Wildlife Resources Commission; Champion International Corporation, Caterpillar Tractor Corporation, West Virginia Paper Corporation, Georgia Pacific, the Weyerhauser Company, and Dr. James W. Hardin, Professor and Curator of the Herbarium, North Carolina State University.

Constructive criticism was given by the late Dr. Anne Adams, Dr. William H. Cartwright, and Dr. Orrin H. Pilkey of the Duke University faculty, and guidance was supplied by the late Dr. Sherwood Githens, Jr., Professor Emeritus, Science Education, Duke University. To these people and organizations, the authors are most grateful.

B. McManus Collins
Fred M. White

chapter 1

Forests: Their Use and Conservation

> *A forest is a community that is as complicated in structure and organization as a community of people, consisting of trees, plants, soils, shrubs, water, and animal life.*

1.1 A "FOREST" DEFINED

It is not the intention of the authors to ask you to learn a burdensome number of technical words. However, it appears advisable at the start to become familiar with a few such words that apply to forestry as a whole.

A forest is a *renewable* resource. It is constantly remaking itself. In a forest the trees and plants make their own food using carbon dioxide from the air and water and *nutrients* from the soil. *Herbivores,* animals that chiefly eat grass and other green plants, may also browse on young trees. *Carnivores,* flesh-eating animals, feed on the herbivores. Then *microorganisms,* fungi and bacteria, decompose the remains of plants and animals into soil substances used by trees and plants. This association of plants, animals, and microorganisms and the nonliving parts, such as water, soil, and chemicals, is known as an *ecosystem.*

A definition of a forest composed by Graves and Guise in 1932 is: "a complex association of trees, shrubs, and other plants in which each individual plays some part in the life of the community." Be-

1

cause a cycle of renewal is absent, nursery plantings and scattered trees in a park are not forests.

1.2 PREHISTORIC USE OF THE FOREST

Whether our primitive ancestors dwelt first in forests, caves, thickets, or primeval "jungles" is a question still studied by anthropologists. Quite likely, human beings evolved in several different environments. Discoveries by archaeologists in several parts of the world have indicated that an environment that was favorable to the development of man consisted of caves located near grassy plains *(savannas)* interspersed with wooded areas.

The problem of early people was to conquer their surroundings; this meant finding safe shelter, food, and warmth. The forest provided all of these. Forests made excellent hunting grounds because dark, protected areas were ideal for the breeding of wild animals. In addition to supplying meat, forests provided fruits, nuts, berries, and roots, which were there just for the gathering. It is likely that forests were where the humanoids learned to hunt animals and use their flesh for food and their pelts for protection and ornamental purposes, and to catch fish in the brooks and streams. The tinder provided by leaves and bark from trees and the grassy roughs may have been the fuel for the first wildfires ignited by burning trees that had been struck by lightning. Thus the first use of fire may be credited to the existence of savannas and forests.

Such a process of human development took place in the temperate nondesert parts of North and South America thousands of years before Eskimos and Indians settled this part of the world. Settlers and explorers from Europe found evidences of earlier civilizations in and along the edges of forests. Medicines were obtained in the forests by the earlier inhabitants: The bark of the Hercules-club tree (also called toothache tree), a small tree of the South, was chewed by victims of toothache for its desensitizing effect on the mouth and gums; a concoction made from the bark of the cinchona tree was found in use as a cure for malaria in the Northern Andes part of South America. A modern antimalarial medicine, quinine, is made from the bark of a tree of the same family.

1.3 FORESTS IN EARLY AMERICAN TIMES

Many American colonists thought of the forest as their enemy. In 1754, Benjamin Franklin and four other Philadelphians made a 5-day trip up the Hudson River from New York to Albany in a sloop (a sailing vessel). His biographer wrote:

> Westward stretched the forest, endless, primeval, reaching on and on. No one in the sloop would have ventured to call the forest beautiful. Rather, it was "solemn, interminable, barbaric, harsh"; one meets these adjectives often. Trees were man's enemy and must be felled. Until they were gone there could be neither crops nor fruit; no safety, no ease, no civilization.[1]

The forests were dense, the trees were large, and many of them were of hard durable wood that would have been almost impossible to dispose of without the use of fire. The land was so completely occupied by these virgin forests with their tangled windfalls, limbs, and tops of trees broken by winds and ice overloads from storms that to clear it for roadways and cultivation was a time-consuming task. In those early days there were few roads. Rafts and boats on waterways such as the great Mississippi and its tributaries were the principal means of travel. The dense forests also provided cover for hostile Indians. Hence, clearing the forests effected protection for settlers as well as making travel and agriculture possible.

The earliest colonists survived by eating wild berries and fruits, shellfish, and the meat of forest animals. Trees felled for farming provided building material and fuel for heat. The earliest homes were made simply of logs and, later, of sawed timber. The food supply shifted later from wild animals to domesticated stock and farm products.

Prior to the start of coal mining in the 1820s and the production of petroleum in the 1860s, wood was the prime fuel used in the United States. The shift away from the use of wood as a fuel was fortunate, because use of wood for many other purposes was being developed.

Early settlers also employed wood to make furniture and tools. Furniture often was more valuable than the house containing it and was harder to replace; for that reason, every member of the firefighting companies started by Benjamin Franklin in Philadelphia was required to own a salvage bag, a wrench with which to unfasten bedsteads, and was under orders to remove valuables before starting to fight a fire.[2]

As the settlers began to use the forests more extensively, even in many instances to the point of exploitation, it became necessary to start some form of forest protection, referred to as *conservation.*

[1] Catherine D. Bowen, *The Most Dangerous Man in America* (Boston: Little Brown & Co., 1974), p. 113.

[2] Patricia Johnston, *Early American Life* (Vol. IX, No. 3, June 1978) p. 31.

1.4 THE DEVELOPMENT OF CONSERVATION

In very early pioneer days, trees were cut down with no thought of replacing them. However, the significance of trees was indicated as early as the 1620s by the Plymouth Colony, when an ordinance was passed prohibiting the felling of timber on any colony land without official consent. A little later in Pennsylvania, William Penn, the governor, ordered that, for every 5 acres of forest land cleared, 1 acre was to be left uncut.

After the United States was established, laws with penalties were passed by several states to prevent thoughtless waste of the forests. In the early 1800s Congress authorized the president to protect live oak and red cedar timber in the state of Florida and to use the Army and Navy for enforcement. During this same period the first step in forestry was taken by the government by providing for the growing of live oaks in the southern states for ship timbers. A federal act also provided for preservation of nearly 250,000 acres of forest land in Florida, Alabama, Mississippi, and Louisiana. According to another act passed in that decade, any person cutting down or destroying living red cedar, live oak, or other trees on federal land could be punished by the government. These laws and regulations, through which the government tried to control the forest land, helped call attention to the importance of forests and led to the development of conservation at the state level.

In January 1867, the first state committee on forest protection was appointed in Michigan, and Wisconsin followed in March of that year. Two years later the State Board of Agriculture of Maine appointed a committee to develop a state policy for the preservation and production of trees. Minnesota created a law in 1871 that granted bounties to encourage the planting of forest trees. The first Arbor Day, a day in late April or early May observed by the planting of trees, was celebrated the following year in Nebraska.

The federal government adopted the Timber Culture Act in the early 1870s. It provided that the government would donate 160 acres of land to any person who planted 40 acres of that area with trees not more than 12 feet apart and kept the trees growing and healthy for one decade. This act, however, was repealed after 10 years because of serious abuses; too many recipients of these grants were not honoring their commitments by failing to follow the rules and regulations pertaining to the grants.

In many instances, while employing fire to prepare their land for cultivation, the settlers disregarded caution relating to neighboring land. Gross carelessness often resulted in destruction of property well beyond the intended burns. An early form of forest protection was the erection of fire towers by the federal and state fire-fighting services for the detection of fires. Because of the high cost of maintenance and salaries, many of the fire towers in the West have been abandoned and detection is now done by observers in aircraft. In the first 50 years of federal, state, and private forestry in the United States, expenditures for protecting forests from fires exceeded all other forestry costs. Since 1945, management activities and research have brought about a more even distribution of expenditures for conservation.

At present about 15 percent of the forests in the United States are under management of some kind. Forest management had to be instituted in order that forests could continue to supply the needs of our increasing population.

1.5 FORESTS AS SOURCES OF LUMBER AND OTHER PRODUCTS

The first sawmill in America was established in Maine in 1623, and within a decade, white pine lumber was being exported to England, where wood was in great demand for construction and repair of ships for the Royal Navy. By order of a Royal charter, trained men were sent over to select and reserve the best, tallest, and straightest pine trees to be used as masts on the king's ships. Colonial woodsmen rebelled against the king's taking their best timber, on which they depended for their livelihood; they took the attitude that they were no longer under the rule of the old country and continued to cut timber for their own use. Also, farmers were upset because they could not clear land for a cornfield if many of the trees bore the king's broad arrow.[3] Those who sold lumber thought that export of this material must be continued no matter who the buyers were. Fierce battles were fought over the cutting of these trees; some disgruntled woodsmen burned down whole sections of forests in order that the British would not get the very best wood.

There was a market for naval stores (tar, pitch, turpentine) employed for sealing seams and cracks, painting, and making other repairs of wooden ships. In the early days there were great forests of beautiful longleaf pine trees in North Carolina's coastal plain. Settlers soon discovered that pine sap would produce naval stores, which were sold

---

[3] A broad arrow consisted of three blazes hacked on the tree trunk, one long and two short, arranged in the shape of an arrow.

to shipbuilders in England and New England. North Carolina got its name "Tarheel State" from this industry. For many years it was more important than the sale of lumber and other forest products, such as staves for casks and potash from wood ashes. The sale of tobacco, fish, and other products was not sufficient to provide for all the colonists' needs.

Westward expansion of the nation started in 1776 and continued modestly through the first third of the nineteenth century, became greatly accelerated in the middle third (the days of Horace Greeley, who coined the phrase "Go west, young man, go west!"), and stayed in full swing until the end of the century. As indicated in the following sections, the existence and use of forests played a large part in that activity.

1.6 THE FORESTS AND NATIONAL EXPANSION

The Preemption Act was passed in 1841. It enabled heads of families to purchase 160 acres of land inexpensively for their own use. The Homestead Act, enacted two decades later, was similar but offered a broader range of benefits. It provided that after 5 years of residence and cultivation the settler could have the land free. Enactment of these two laws encouraged settlement of new land, but it also brought about heavy cutting of forests. As the settlers moved west, the forests in those areas were cut down for housing, fences, cropland, and roadways.

In 1850 the first railroad land-grant act was passed to subsidize the construction of railroads. It provided that railroads were to have, in addition to an adequate right of way, a free portion of land, which included each alternate square mile or section in a band 6 miles wide on each side of the road. Such generous laws led to some unforeseen results. During the last half of the nineteenth century, railroads received 200 million acres of land from the U. S. government, much of which bore some of the finest timber in the United States. A large part of it was sold for sawtimber.

As a result of the land grants, the nation received several transcontinental railroad lines. People were able to travel farther, faster, and with greater ease. Towns and cities grew and, of course, trade and commerce also. Hence need was created for additional lumber. Nearly 29,000 sawmills were in full production by 1870, and the annual forest harvest was nearly 13 billion board feet of lumber, enough to build 650,000 homes. (One board foot represents a volume of wood that is 12 inches long, 12 inches wide, and 1 inch thick.)

With the continuing increase in population, there was more need for wood. By the turn of the twentieth century, 90,000 family farms were being established annually. The demands for lumber for the construction and maintenance of farms, towns, and cities were increasing, and timber supplies became low.

1.7   BRIEF HISTORY OF TIMBER HARVESTING AND USE

The forests of early America were vast. In Arkansas, for example, there were only about 1,000 acres of open land; all the rest was heavily forested. It was said of Ohio that a squirrel could cross the whole state leaping from tree to tree, so dense was the hardwood forest that covered it. The sandy soils of the Lakes States supported extensive stands of eastern white and red pines. The far West had incredible coniferous forests, as yet unexplored.

These extensive forests were a mixed blessing, for to the farmer they were an obstacle to be overcome; yet at the same time they supported a thriving lumber industry, which supplied the material to build the cities, ships, railroads, and bridges of a nation. As the nation's population grew and expanded westward, the demand for forest products expanded with it. The use of the forests is a rich part of American history.

The lumber industry began in New England, in the spruce and white pine forests. Here the heavy winter snows and numerous fast-moving rivers combined to provide both easy transportation and a source of power to the water-powered sawmills. As logging and milling efficiency increased, the forest margins were pushed farther back from the rivers. This fact, plus shifting population, prompted the development of heavy logging activities in New York, Pennsylvania, West Virginia, and Virginia. Here too the virgin forests melted away before the expanding farmlands and cities.

Still the population moved westward, and the lumber industry followed it. In the mid-1800s the pine forests of the Lakes States were being cut at an accelerating rate to provide lumber to build the midwestern villages, towns, and cities. Railroads came into use, first to transport lumber to eastern markets, and then to move logs from the forests to sawmills. The legend of Paul Bunyan grew from this region and this time. As the forests were cut and abandoned and as destructive forest fires swept vast areas, a feeling of concern over the waste and initial fears of timber shortages gradually arose. From these concerns the conservation movement was born, and also from them the profession of forestry ultimately developed.

After most of the easily accessible stands of the Lakes States were cut by about 1920, peak lumber production shifted to the pine forests of the Southeast. Here the gentle terrain and a climate that permits year-round logging resulted in the production of a massive volume of structural lumber in a very brief period of years. Many early southern fortunes were made from forests. Railroad logging was perfected, and cable-skidding techniques were developed to hasten the flow of logs from the forests to the mills. In less than 20 years the extensive forests of longleaf, slash, and shortleaf pines had been reduced to a mere remnant. Many of the sawmills were dismantled and moved to the northwestern states.

However, a few of the early lumbermen stayed behind and found that the pines of the South, particularly the loblolly pine, replace themselves more rapidly than do the trees in the regions that had been logged earlier in the North. They found that leaving a number of the better trees to reseed the cutover land is an effective means of establishing a young and vigorous forest. This practice marked the beginning of industrial forestry in the United States.

On a modest scale, logging and milling had begun many years earlier in the awe-inspiring forests of the Northwest. However, the immense size of the trees, the primitive nature of the available tools, and the fact that to reach eastern markets lumber had to be shipped around the southern tip of South America all served to restrain the logging industry. The establishment of transcontinental railroads, the opening of the Panama Canal, and the equipment skills learned in the South removed these restraints. From the 1920s on, the western forests have produced more lumber than any of the other forest regions of the country. Because of the rough terrain and large tree sizes, it was here that the mechanical processes of logging progressed most rapidly. The use of large crawler tractors, railroads, and trucks and elaborate systems for transporting logs in water chutes or by intricate systems of overhead cables were developed to high efficiency.

After the westward movement of the lumber industry came the expansion of the pulp and paper industry. Paper was first made from wood in North America in 1867. By the early 1900s, paper mills dotted the Northeast and the Lakes States. Later a process suitable for pulping the resinous southern pines was developed, and this region quickly moved to the forefront in paper production. Today it is a major national industry, and the annual demand for more than 25 million tons of wood pulp has caused it to become a leader in the practice of intensive scientific forestry.

Plywood has become an important forest product. It is a wood sandwich made of sheets of veneer (very thin slices of wood) with an

Figure 1–1. Plywood being manufactured in a mill at Jacksonville, North Carolina. (Courtesy the Weyerhaeuser Company)

odd number of sheets glued together with the grain in a criss-cross arrangement. Figure 1–1 shows plywood being manufactured in a mill in Jacksonville, North Carolina.

1.8 SUMMARY

A forest is a complex community and a renewable resource. Since prehistoric times, forests have been important to humanity. They have provided food for humans from animals and berries, shelter, and forest products—commodities people can use. In colonial days the forests were very extensive, and their presence, in addition to being useful, was a hazard and a detriment to the start of agriculture.

Lumbering had its start in America in 1623. Originally, wood was used for fuel, building material, and construction of furniture. Today, heat and steam energy are derived largely from other sources, so wood is used mainly as building material and for various other products such as paper. American ingenuity is resulting in newer and better ways to use the available wood.

Need for conservation was seen soon after the nation was formed, but for a long time few active steps were taken. Serious effort began about a century ago. An early step was development of fire detection and suppression. Reforestation has become a major part of conservation, and forests are now being managed scientifically and intelligently and are one of the major assets of our nation. The hasty and wasteful cutting of forests that accompanied the westward movement of people in the nineteenth century is now a thing of the past.

The northern, southern, and northwestern forest regions have each in turn led the country in the production of forest products. Today all these forest regions support a high level of forestry activity. This level must increase in all regions if the nation's growing need for the many products of the forest are to be met for future generations.

chapter 2

Forests of the United States

2.1 THE ORIGINAL FORESTS

When America was discovered by Europeans, much of what is now the eastern United States was covered with trees, which, except for slight modifications by the Indians, had never been disturbed by people. Forests extended nearly unbroken along the eastern seaboard of the continent and westward across it for hundreds of miles.

About the year 986 A.D. when Bjarni Heriulfsson sailed out from Iceland to go to the new Norse colony on Greenland (an island located to the east of Canada), winds raged upon the sea and the sun and stars were blotted out. Bjarni trimmed the sail of his long-boat and scudded before the storm. So it was that he came to a new land that was "level and covered with woods."[1]

There is general belief that about the year 1,000, the Greenlander, Leif, "The Lucky" Ericsson, landed with his crew of Norsemen on the mainland somewhere near New England or to the north of it and

[1] Ovid Butler, comp. and ed., *American Conservation*, 4th ed. (Washington, D.C.: American Forestry Association, 1941), p. 16.

described a region "of rolling hills and plenty of trees." They made use of the forests to repair their boats and took grapes and samples of timber back to Greenland, a land that had wild animals for food and fur but few large trees. A few years later Leif and his crews returned to the mainland at what we now call Labrador and built a logging camp. Hence, forest products were the first goods taken from this continent.

Following the journeys of the courageous Vikings, other explorers visited this continent. Some were in search of gold, others sought furs and spices, while still others came looking for timber and naval stores. These last two needs were most important in colonial times, for transportation was almost entirely by water and the growing commerce of the new world called for ships. One of the main reasons given for settling Jamestown was Britain's hope of developing a source of naval stores. To make money, some English business groups familiar with the growing demands for forest products sponsored some of the colonies. These colonies were under a constant threat: If they did not make money for these enterprising groups, their supplies would be stopped and they would have to return to England. Fortunately, these business ventures resulted in permanent settlements, even though the colonists suffered hardships.

Near the center of the United States, because of scanty rainfall, the forests become open and scrubby and finally disappear in the Great Plains, millions of acres of grasslands. Beyond the plains lies another forest region, which consists of two parts, one extending through the Rocky Mountains, the other throughout the Sierra Nevada and Cascade Mountains and ending at the Pacific Ocean.

2.2 FOREST REGIONS OF THE UNITED STATES

United States forests consist of 860 species (kinds) of trees, many of which are of economic significance. Our forest lands, totaling about 762 million acres, are in several large regions that are mapped in Figures 2-1, 2-2, and 2-3. Commercial forests from which our lumber, paper, and other forest products come make up about two thirds of these wooded regions. Noncommercial forests account for the other third. These are wooded areas that are inaccessible or economically impractical to harvest. They include hard-to-reach swamplands, mountain lands, and areas that do not grow useful timber. In addition, parks, wilderness land, and game refuges are considered noncommercial.

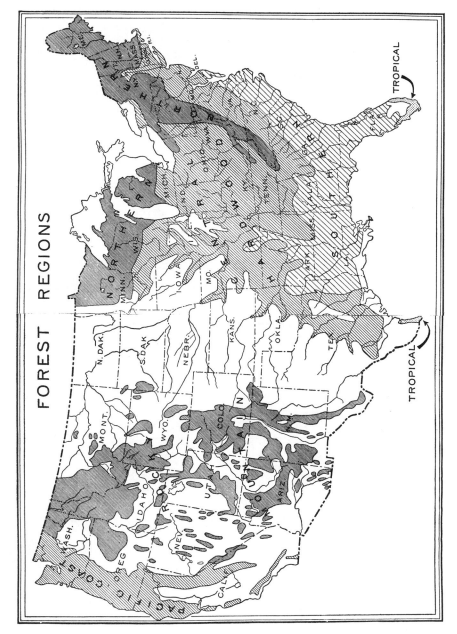

Figure 2-1. Forest regions of the continental United States. (Courtesy USDA Forest Service)

Figure 2-2. Forest regions in Alaska. (Courtesy USDA Forest Service)

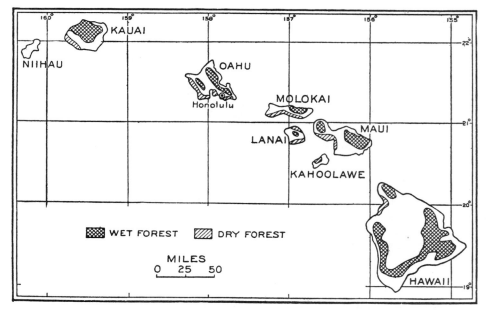

Figure 2-3. Forests in Hawaii. (Courtesy USDA Forest Service)

Because of differences in temperature, moisture, and conditions of the soil, not every kind of tree can grow in every region. Figure 2-1 shows, from east to west, six forest regions in the continental United States: northern (or eastern), central, southern, tropical, Rocky Mountain (or western), and Pacific coast. Each consists of various forest types composed of different species grouped in natural associations or communities (ecosystems). Altitude affects climate, and this accounts for the extension of the ranges of some northern trees into southern mountains both in the east and west. Figures 2-2 and 2-3 identify the prevailing forest regions in Alaska and Hawaii. The forests of Hawaii, present on seven of the major islands, are of both wet and dry types.

Shifts in the patterns of land use have resulted in alterations in forest types. For example, in the last few decades, many oak and pine stands in the southern forest region have been converted to pine stands by killing or cutting hardwoods, followed by the planting of pines. Other rather extensive modifications of our forest areas have come about because of growth in population and industry.

2.3 THE NORTHERN OR EASTERN FOREST REGION

The northern forest region covers all the northeastern United States, extending as far west as the Lakes States, and includes most of Michigan, Wisconsin, and Minnesota. It stretches southward through the Appalachian Mountains to northern Georgia. The forests in this region once made up more than one eighth of all the forest land in the United States but have been reduced by population and industrial growth. The northern forest region is characterized by temperate mixed forests of coniferous and deciduous species and cool coniferous forests.

The evergreens, including most conifers, which do not shed all their leaves annually, are the major trees of the northern forest region. Some evergreens that represent the region are eastern white pine, red, black, and white spruce, Norway or red pine, jack pine, balsam fir, white cedar, and eastern hemlock. Some deciduous species (hardwood or broad-leaved trees) of importance found in the northern forests are beech, northern red oak, white oak, aspen, yellow birch, paper birch, black birch, black walnut, sugar maple, black gum, white ash, black cherry, and basswood. Deciduous species shed their leaves annually.

Chestnut trees once formed a large portion of the total stand in the northern forests and the adjacent central hardwood forest, but because of a fungal blight in the early twentieth century the species has been nearly eliminated as a tree and is now a minor species of the understory. Chestnuts remain only as sprouts from old stumps, and these live for only about 10 years. An occasional tree is still found to have escaped the blight.

The commercial forest land of this region amounts to 115 million acres, and it yields about 15 percent of the lumber and about 26 percent of the pulpwood produced in the United States.

2.4 THE CENTRAL FOREST REGION

The central hardwood region covers a large area of the central portion of the eastern half of the United States. As indicated in Figure 2-1, it is located between the northern and southern forest regions. It stretches westward from Connecticut to southern Minnesota; southward, not including the southern Appalachian Mountains, through the Piedmont, the Cumberland plateau, to northern parts of Georgia, Alabama, and Mississippi; and through Arkansas to eastern Oklahoma and central Texas. This region extends over a greater area than any other of the great forests of America. But like the northern region, this area has been reduced greatly to make way for population, agricultural, and industrial growth.

The principal trees of this region are hardwoods (Figure 2-4). The central forests include northern red oak, hickory, beech, elm, red maple, white ash, sycamore, cottonwood, black walnut, black gum, yellow poplar, and sweet or red gum. The central region has more different species of trees than any other forest region of the United States. The conifers represented in the central region include several pines: Virginia, shortleaf, pitch, and eastern red cedar, and occasionally eastern hemlocks. The 139 million acres of commercial forest in the central region produce approximately 5 percent of our lumber and nearly 10 percent of the pulpwood of the United States.

2.5 THE SOUTHERN FOREST REGION

Often called the yellow pine forest, the southern forest region covers most of the states in the southeastern part of the United States, as indicated in Figure 2-1. It lies south of the northern region and borders on the Atlantic Ocean, beginning with southern Delaware and extending southward to, but not including, the southern tip of Florida. It stretches west along the Gulf plains to eastern Texas, north to Okla-

Figure 2-4. Mixed hardwood forest: oak, yellow poplar, maple, and gum in a central hardwood forest. (Courtesy USDA Forest Service)

homa, and up the Mississippi Valley into southern Missouri and Illinois. The southern region comprises about one third of America's forests and is potentially the most important timber-producing area of the United States. Even though southern pines are among its most important trees, the southern region is also one of hardwoods. It has swamps with dense growths of red maple, black gum or tupelo, bald cypress (a conifer), and other species of significant value. Figure 2-5 shows a mixed black tupelo and cypress swamp, with "knees," outgrowths of the cypress roots, projecting above the water surface. Figure 2-6 shows a mixed hardwood forest of oak, yellow poplar, maple, and gum, with an oak of commercial size being marked with paint for harvest. The region has a particularly large number of oaks, yellow poplars, maples, and walnuts. Other broad-leaved or hardwood species found in the southern region are white ash, cottonwood, hickory, and pecan.

The pine trees in the southern region are primarily loblolly, shortleaf, slash, longleaf, and Virginia. Figure 2-7 shows a longleaf seedling beginning height growth in a young stand of longleaf pines. Pitch and pond pines occur also, but to a limited extent. Figure 2-8 shows a southern pine forest in which selective cupping (removal of

Figure 2-5. Mixed black tupelo and cypress swamp in a southern forest, showing "knees" projecting above water surface. (Courtesy USDA Forest Service)

Figure 2-6. Tree-marking paint and gun in use in a southern hardwood forest. (Courtesy USDA Forest Service)

Figure 2-7. A young longleaf pine tree. (Courtesy USDA Forest Service)

Figure 2-8. Selectively cut slash pine forest with cupping for naval stores in progress. (Courtesy USDA Forest Service)

sap) for naval stores is in progress. Longleaf and slash pine are the two principal naval stores species. The southern forests have maintained the naval stores industry for the three centuries and have given the United States the distinction of world leadership in producing these products. Many naval stores products are now produced as by-products of the pulping of southern pines by the paper industry.

The southern forest region has a commercial forest area of 166 million acres. It produces approximately 27 percent of all U.S. lumber, better than 45 percent of the pulpwood, and about 25 percent of all the plywood produced in this country.

2.6 TROPICAL FORESTS

The tropical forests of the continental United States, which actually are more subtropical than tropical, are located in two restricted areas: at the southern tip of Florida and in a small section of southeastern Texas, as is indicated in Figure 2–1. These forests, typified by the Florida Everglades, make up the smallest forest region in America. The principal trees of this region, mahogany, mangrove, and bay, are all broad-leaved species. The palm and mangrove (evergreen trees and shrubs) of these forests form dense thickets in tidal creeks and estuaries. Though the trees of these tropical forests are commercially unimportant, the mangroves are ecologically very significant. They produce a network of long stiltlike roots that grow in the mud. Debris and soil particles washed in by the tides lodge in these roots. After many years the shore line is extended by the buildup of this material. The tropical forest regions of the United States in both Florida and southern Texas have no commercial forest areas. The forests of Hawaii, as illustrated by Figure 2–11, though small in area, are extremely important as a source of fiber and for watershed and recreation purposes.

2.7 THE ROCKY MOUNTAIN OR WESTERN REGION

The western region spreads over the slopes and high plateaus of the Rocky Mountains. It extends from Canada down to Mexico, and west from the great prairies to the Great Basin between the Rocky Mountains and the Cascade and Sierra Nevada mountains of the Far West, as indicated in Figure 2–1. The evergreens are important trees in this forest region and western pines of economic significance are found here: the ponderosa, western white, and lodgepole. Mixed in with the pines and growing over smaller areas one finds Engelmann spruce, Douglas fir, western larch, western red cedar, white fir, and western hemlock. Aspen is the major broad-leaved tree in this forest region.

This region is characterized by isolated forest areas or patches largely because of great differences in land elevations. At the higher elevations the western forest resembles islands of trees bordered at their bases by broad valleys of treeless lowlands and above by barren mountain tops too high for tree growth. The stretches of treeless lowlands within these areas are mostly natural prairies and grasslands used for grazing cattle and sheep. The commerical forest part of the western forest region, consisting of 73 million acres, produces about 27 percent of U.S. lumber.

2.8   THE PACIFIC COAST FOREST REGION

The Pacific coast region lies west of the Great Basin and extends south from British Columbia through western Washington and Oregon and to the San Francisco Bay area of California, as shown in Figure 2-1. Today only one third of the original forest exists, but it still is a very significant forest. The commercial part amounts to 48 million acres, which produces 27 percent of all U.S. lumber, 19 percent of all U.S. pulpwood, and 75 percent of all the plywood.

The dominant trees in the Pacific coast forests are evergreens. Among them are the largest trees in the world: the magnificent redwoods that tower to heights of more than 300 feet and the giant sequoias that have trunks that measure as much as 30 feet in diameter, which were named after the ingenious creator of the Cherokee alphabet, Sequoyah.

Douglas fir, one of the nation's most important commercial trees, grows here and in the Rocky Mountain region. The Douglas fir and ponderosa pine areas collectively make up 6 percent of the commercial timberland in the United States. The most extensive commercial forest type in California and the Rocky Mountains is the ponderosa pine. Other conifers of the Pacific coast region that have commercial value are western hemlock, western red cedar, Sitka spruce, sugar pine, lodgepole pine, incense cedar, noble fir, and white fir. Broad-leaved trees of economic significance in this region are red alder, big-leaf maple, a variety of oaks, and black cottonwood. Figure 2-9 is a view of a second-growth redwood showing stump sprouts in a western coastal forest. Figure 2-10 shows a stand of Douglas fir in Oregon.

Figure 2-9. Second-growth coast redwood showing stump sprouts. (Courtesy USDA Forest Service)

Figure 2-10. Douglas fir growing in Toledo, Oregon. (Courtesy USDA Forest Service)

The Alaskan forest region, shown in Figure 2–2, is divided into two areas, the coastal and the interior. The coastal forest extends from the southeastern portion of Alaska (along the south coast through the Kenai peninsula) to Kodiak Island. All the important tree species in the coastal forest are conifers: Sikta spruce, western hemlock, Alaska yellow cedar, and western red cedar. Sitka spruce and western hemlock are the principal species of commercial importance. This forest area has 6 million acres of commercial forest land that produce lumber and pulpwood.

Important tree species of the Alaskan interior forest region are black and white spruce (conifers) and aspen and white birch (hardwoods). Black spruce is common along streams, lake shores, flood plains, and other well-drained lowlands. Other hardwoods found in the interior are cottonwood, alder, and willow. The interior forest consists of 105 million acres, and because of the high cost of transporting lumber from the interior to the coast, most of this wood is used for local enterprises.

The forested parts of Hawaii are also classified into two regions, wet forest and dry forest. These extend over one half of the land area

Figure 2–11. A typical palm and evergreen wet forest in Hawaii. (Courtesy USDA Forest Service)

of the seven main islands, as indicated in Figure 2–3. Niihau, the eighth island, has no forests. The leading species in the wet forests are all broad-leaved trees. These are ohia, boa, tree fern, kukui, tropical ash, mamani, and eucalyptus. These trees are used for lumber, furniture, and souvenirs. Production is negligible. There are 1 million acres in the commercial part of the wet forests.

The main species of the dry forests are koa, haole, algaroba, monkey pod, and wiliwili. These are used locally for fuel wood and fence posts. There is no commercial forest growth in the dry-forest area of Hawaii.

2.10 SUMMARY

When explorers and early expeditions came to North America, its forests were its most apparent resource. Over half of the country was forested, and early settlers had the mistaken belief that the forest was inexhaustible. The commercial market for forest products formed an incentive for the establishment of settlements.

America's forests are diverse in species. Certain types of trees predominate in various geographical regions, because of differences in temperature, moisture supply, soil conditions, and elevation.

The forests of the eastern United States, which differ considerably from those of the western part, are classified into the northern, central, southern, and tropical regions. They consist of a wide distribution of both softwoods and hardwoods of commercial importance, except in the tropical region. Favorable climatic conditions account for this wide distribution of prominent commercial species.

The forest regions west of the Great Plains are classified into the western or Rocky Mountain, Pacific coast, Alaskan, and Hawaiian regions. The western and Pacific coast regions have a variety of softwoods of high commercial value, but few important hardwoods. The commercial hardwoods of the western forests are much less extensive than those in the eastern forests.

chapter 3

Some Commercially Important Trees

3.1 IDENTIFICATION OF TREES

Trees are woody plants, but all woody plants are not trees. A tree usually grows upright to at least 20 feet (15.5 meters) at maturity and has a single stem, often called *bole* or *trunk*. The stem supports limbs and leaves, forming the *top* or *crown*. Other woody plants are vines and shrubs. Vines may have woody stems but do not have a distinct crown of upright branches. Shrubs may have several woody stems growing from a clump, and they usually are smaller than trees.

Trees generally develop a typical shape when they grow in an open area. Figure 3-1 shows a white oak that grew in the open, while Figure 3-2 shows a young white oak that has a long clear trunk, which was attained while competing for light in a closed forest, before the crowding trees were cut to make way for a new road. Trees that grow in crowded forests usually have trunks of greater clear length. Essentially, we have no timberline resulting from high elevation in the East, but at timberline and at higher mountain elevations in the West many trees are knurled, twisted, and sometimes

Figure 3-1. (*Left*) White oak grown in the open. (Courtesy USDA Forest Service)

Figure 3-2. (*Right*) White oak that grew crowded among other trees. (Courtesy USDA Forest Service)

prostrate, as illustrated by the bristlecone pine in Figure 3–3, which represents trees that grow on very adverse sites. Such tortuous form is the result of many factors, including thin soils, limited growth periods, deep snows, and continuous exposure to strong winds. However, under favorable conditions, most species develop characteristic shapes. Several field trips with a good identification manual showing local species should enable an inexperienced person to become rather proficient in identifying trees.

Identification features are also found in bud, flower, fruit, leaf, twig, and bark structure. The precise botanical characteristics by which trees are classified (primarily flower parts) are too small or fleeting to be useful in field identification for those with little experience. The gross features (shape, leaf and bark structure, buds and twigs) are more useful for quick field identification.

Trees and other plants often have several common names, which vary with locality or local usage. To make specific identities worldwide, botanists employ Latinized names, which remain constant since

Figure 3-3. Dead bristlecone pine. (Courtesy USDA Forest Service)

Latin is a language that no longer changes. The scientific name consists of two parts: the *genus* (a collection of closely related species) and the *specific epithet* or species (a collection of individuals so similar that they suggest common parentage and produce like off-spring). The generic name always appears first and is capitalized, while the specific name follows and begins with a lowercase letter.[1]

Because general and regional guides to field identification of trees and government publications that describe local or native trees are readily available, only a few of the important commercially significant trees of the major forest regions will be studied in this chapter. Most of these are valued for their wood products.

Prior to studying individual tree species, it is necessary to know that trees are divided into two main groups. These are the conifers (*gymnosperms*) or softwood trees and the broadleaf (*angiosperms*) or hardwood trees. Conifers have mostly needlelike or scalelike leaves and bear their seeds in cones or conzlike structures. The

---

[1] W.M. Harlow, E.S. Harrar, and Fred M. White, *Textbook of Dendrology* 6th ed. (New York: McGraw-Hill Book Co., 1979), pp. 10–13.

conifers or evergreens do not shed all their leaves annually, with the exception of larch and bald cypress. Deciduous trees, those that shed all their leaves in the fall, generally are broad-leaved hardwoods.

The terms hardwood and softwood can be misleading because the wood of some hardwood trees is softer than that of some softwood trees. For example, the wood of yellow poplar and basswood is much softer than that of the longleaf pine.

We will first study the conifers, which are widely distributed in the various regions and are very significant in the production of lumber and paper.

3.2 LONGLEAF PINE *(PINUS PALUSTRIS)*

Longleaf pine is one of the most important and historically distinctive southern conifers. It was among the first trees cut in the colonial years. This pine and the loblolly, plus white pine of the North, supplied masts for ships that sailed the high seas. In those early years it was the chief source of our naval stores. The wood of the longleaf pine is strong, durable, and good for many purposes. It has long been used for construction purposes. Longleaf pine is easy to cut and haul because these trees grow in pure stands on dry, level sites. It is confined to a belt along the South Atlantic and Gulf Coastal plains. Originally, there were large forests of longleaf pine with distributions from near sea level up to a 1,900-feet (580 meters) altitude in the Appalachian Mountains of Alabama. Today, only remnants remain in the uplands.

Longleaf pine is relatively easy to identify because its needles and cones are the longest of any southern pine. The needles are 8 to 18 inches (20–46 cm) in length and usually grow in bundles (*fascicles*) of three. They are bright green and on older trees densely tufted at the ends of stout branch tips. Except during the early growing season, longleaf pine can be recognized by its large candlelike white buds. Mature trees have cones 6 to 10 (15–25 cm) inches long with spine-tipped scales. The cones are reddish brown, weathering to an ashy gray. The longleaf pine (Figure 3–4) is a medium-sized to large tree 75 to 120 feet (25 to 36 meters) tall and from 2 to nearly 3 feet (60 to 85 centimeters) in diameter. It has a long clear trunk with dark reddish brown mature bark in rough, scaly plates, and has a sparse open crown. The root system consists of a very deep taproot with many wide-spreading, well-developed lateral roots.

Longleaf pine is quite *shade intolerant*; it does not grow well in the shade of larger trees. Young trees grow slowly, forming deep

Figure 3-4. Longleaf pines in a park area. (Courtesy USDA Forest Service)

roots. For the first few years they form only a tuft of foliage; this is known as the "grass stage." In this grass stage this species is exceptionally resistant to fires, and also after it has reached a height of 12 to 15 feet (3 to 5 meters). Longleaf pine grows best in the open on deep, well-drained, acidic, sandy soils. It regenerates more slowly than other pines after a harvesting. Currently, after forest industry harvests most longleaf sites, large areas are replanted with loblolly and/or slash pine by mechanical planters or by hand.

Longleaf pine is valuable for lumber, poles, piling, plywood, pulpwood, and, as previously mentioned, naval stores.

3.3 LOBLOLLY PINE *(PINUS TAEDA)*

Loblolly pine is the leading commercial timber species in the South. Growing best in low, moist areas, it is found in abundance in the coastal plain and Piedmont. As a result of its prolific seeding and fast growth rate, it becomes established quickly on fields that once were cultivated. Hence, it is often referred to as "old field" pine. The term "loblolly" was used by early settlers to describe a moist depression or mudhole, and this term is descriptive of the tree's

Figure 3-5. Loblolly pine that was crowded in early life and thus losts its lower branches. (Courtesy USDA Forest Service)

habitat. Even though loblolly grows on a wide variety of soils, it does best on those having deep surface layers and abundant moisture.

Needles of the loblolly pine are from 6 to 9 inches (15 to 23 centimeters) in length and in bundles of three, rarely two or four. The yellow-green needles are slender, stiff, and sometimes twisted. The cones are 3 to 6 inches (7 to 15 centimeters) long, and each cone scale has a distinct prickle on its edge. When loblolly grows in a forest, it has a long clear trunk that supports a crown denser than that of other southern pines. The bark of older loblollys is ¾ to 2 inches (2-5 cm) thick, with irregular reddish-brown plates. The trees have relatively short taproots, but an extensive lateral root system.

Loblolly pine is a medium to large tree 80 to 110 feet (25 to 35 meters) in height and from 2 to 3 feet (60 to 90 centimeters) in diameter. Figure 3-5 shows a loblolly that grew in a closed stand and was crowded in early life; it self-pruned well (lost its early branches) and had only a small crown when the nearby trees were cut. Pure stands (stands all of one species) of loblolly can develop almost anywhere this tree grows. Loblolly occurs on so many sites that it is often found growing with a large number of other species, including other southern pines. Loblolly and southern hardwoods are common associates in many forest stands. Loblolly is more shade tolerant than longleaf and slash pine, but less tolerant than its hardwood associates.

Loblolly pine is valuable for lumber, poles, pilings, plywood, and pulpwood. More than one-fourth of the pulpwood produced in the United States comes from southern pines, and a large percentage of this is loblolly. It is currently the most widely planted and intensively managed of all southern species.

3.4 SHORTLEAF PINE *(PINUS ECHINATA)*

The ability of shortleaf pine to grow on a variety of soils probably accounts for its wide distribution. Although it is found on many different sites, shortleaf pine is most common in pure or mixed stands on dry upland soils, such as rolling hills and red soils, that are neither highly alkaline or acidic. Shortleaf is found in the northern, central, and southern forest regions. It is the major hard pine in the central region and in the Appalachian uplands, and again in Missouri, Oklahoma, and parts of Kansas. Shortleaf is often found in stands mixed with hardwood which eventually replaces it.

Shortleaf pine is often difficult to recognize; its needles are among the shortest of the southern pines, and such is the origin of its name. The dark yellow-green, slender, and flexible needles are 3 to 5 inches (7 to 13 centimeters) long and are mostly in bundles of two, but also of three on the same tree. The cones are very small, 1.5 to 2.5 inches (4 to 6 centimeters) long, and each scale is tipped with a prickle. The bark is reddish brown and in irregular, scaly plates that feature numerous small, round, shallow holes.

Figure 3-6 shows a mature shortleaf pine that is 140 years old, 102 feet (32 meters) high, and 26 inches (66 centimeters) in diameter, growing in a mixed stand of evergreens and hardwoods. Trees of this species range from 80 to 100 feet (24 to 35 meters) in height and 2 to 3 feet (61 to 91 centimeters) in diameter. The well-formed trunk supports a narrow, pyramidlike crown and has a very deep taproot. Shortleaf pine is less shade tolerant than loblolly and grows vigorously when released from surrounding trees. Though its growth is slow, it is noted for the duration of this growth.

The wood of shortleaf pine is valuable for lumber, plywood, poles, and pulpwood.

3.5 CYPRESS *(TAXODIUM DISTICHUM)*

Bald cypress, including pond cypress, like the redwoods, is of ancient lineage. It attains large size and reaches an impressive age. Bald

Figure 3-6. (*Left*) A mature shortleaf pine in the Ovachita National Forest, Arkansas. (Courtesy USDA Forest Service)

Figure 3-7. (*Right*) Bald cypress in Ocala National Forest, Florida. (Courtesy USDA Forest Service)

cypress is found along the coastal plain from southern Delaware to South Florida, and west through southeastern Texas nearly to the Mexican border. Cypress is also very common in the Mississippi Valley and as far north as Illinois. Large forests of cypress once covered much of the coastal swampland in the coastal plain along the many streams of the southeastern states. Most if not all of the virgin cypress forests have been cut. Bald cypress grows on soils consisting of clays or the finer sands where moisture is fairly permanent and on swamp soils that are neither acid or alkaline.

This tree is reasonably easy to recognize by three rather prominent distinguishing features: As shown in Figure 3-7, the tree has a swollen or buttressed butt, tiny leaflets, and woody "knees" that protrude between a few inches and several feet above the water from a shallow, wide-spreading lateral root system. The bald cypress grows 100 to 125 feet (30 to 37 meters) tall and 3 to 5 feet (90 to 150 centimeters) in diameter. Cypress is said to be intermediate in shade tolerance. The leaves and cones of cypress are very small. Linear needles not much more than ½ inch (1.3 cm) long grow on lateral branchlets. The wrinkled, round cones, approximately 1 (2.54 cm) inch in diameter, mature in one-season and then disintegrate. The leaves of cypress are shed each fall, which makes it the only conifer in the southern forest that is not an evergreen. The trunk, which supports a pyramidal or in some cases irregular crown, has an ash-gray to reddish-brown fibrous or scaly bark. This tree is often seen with Spanish moss draped from its limbs.

Extensive use of cypress was not made, except locally, until the 1870s when development of transcontinental railways made it available to people throughout the United States. Cypress wood is valuable because it is very durable and for this reason has been labeled "wood everlasting" or "wood eternal." On the basis of its resistance to dampness and other weather conditions, it is highly desired for boats, weather boarding for houses, fence posts and fence rails, and other applications that require durability.

3.6 EASTERN WHITE PINE *(PINUS STROBUS L.)*

Of all the conifers of the northern forest, none is more well known than white pine. This stately tree, the tallest of all the conifers in eastern North America, was the basis of the early forest industry of the North. Growing to immense sizes and occurring in dense stands, it furnished light but strong masts; structural timbers; wide, clear, easily worked boards; and roof shingles for both export and local use. The range of white pine is from New England westward across the Lakes States to central Minnesota and southwesterly down the Appalachian ridge to northern Georgia. Today within this range it is the conifer most utilized for forestry activity.

White pine seedlings are quite small, and for the first 3 or so years growth is very slow. This period is followed by a gradual acceleration to very rapid height growth which has been known to reach 4 feet (1.22 meters) per year. Trees 220 feet (67.1 meters) tall and 6 feet (1.83 meters) in diameter have been noted.

White pine begins to produce seed at an early age and is very aggressive in reproducing itself, especially on abandoned farmlands and disturbed sites. Its seedlings and saplings are moderately shade tolerant, but it becomes less tolerant as it grows older. In the open it does not prune itself well and often is covered with branches, but in dense stands it ultimately produces straight, branch-free stems.

Aggressive reproduction, rapid growth, and high-quality wood have made this the most managed pine of the northern forest. The white pine blister rust and a root rotting disease caused by the *Fomes* fungus are serious diseases. The white pine weevil, which deforms by repeatedly destroying growing tips, is a major insect pest in the North.

The distinctive blue-green needles are 3 to 5 inches (8 to 13 centimeters) long and are in bundles of five per fasicle. The cones are 4 to 8 inches (10 to 20 centimeters) long, slender, often slightly curved, and have no spines on the scales. The bark of new twigs is of a distinctive orange-brown color. The stem bark of young trees is smooth and dark green, while the bark on old stems is gray, thick, and deeply furrowed. The orderly one whorl of branches each year is obscured in the mature tree (Figure 3–8). As the tree grows older the branches fall away and prune themselves. The bark then grows over the knots left by the branches that have been pruned by winds or the force of gravity and it becomes very difficult to determine the age of older trees.

3.7 PONDEROSA PINE *(PINUS PONDEROSA)*

The range of ponderosa pine stretches from North Dakota to western Oregon and California and south well into Mexico. It is found from sea level to 9,000-feet (2700 meters) elevation. In part because of this vast range, more ponderosa pine is harvested for lumber than any other pine species in America. Its wood, unlike that of other hard pines, is often soft and even grained, and this in part accounts for its extreme popularity for lumber.

Rainfall is scarce throughout much of its range, and consequently ponderosa has developed a high level of drought resistance. Among a number of reasons for this is its ability to develop deep-reaching roots very early. A 1-year-old seedling may be less than 3 inches (8 centimeters) tall and yet have a taproot nearly 2 feet (61 centimeters) long.

Ponderosa can become very large (see Figure 3–9). The record size is 8½ feet (2.6 meters) in diameter and 232 feet (71 meters) tall. Throughout most of its range it is a very slow growing tree. This is due largely to dry conditions, for where moisture is available ponderosa can grow as rapidly as most other hard pines. Some trees live to be 600 years old, and one has been known to have lived for 726 years.

Figure 3-8. (*Left*) Mature white pine in mixed northern forest in Wisconsin (Courtesy USDA Forest Service)

Figure 3-9. (*Right*) A stately ponderosa pine in California. It is 74 inches at d.b.h. and contains about 20,000 board feet. (Courtesy USDA Forest Service)

Reproduction is irregular and usually occurs when rare summer rainfalls follow good seed crops. This often results in very dense young stands with so many crowded stems that none grow well. These are called stagnated stands and are a serious problem for forest managers throughout much of the West.

Ponderosa pine is moderately shade tolerant as a seedling and can exist in the understory for several decades. It grows less tolerant with age. It is very resistant to damage by fire and can survive all but the most intense wildfires.

The yellow-green needles of ponderosa are in bundles of two and three and are about 7 inches (18 centimeters) long. These features, plus cones that are about 4 inches (10 centimeters) long, serve to distinguish this species from all but one of the other western pines. The bark on young trees is dark brown to almost black and is very rough. As the tree grows older, the bark forms wide, smooth, irregularly shaped plates that are yellow-brown to rusty red in color. An open, parklike stand of large red-barked ponderosa pines is one of the most attractive sights in the West.

3.8 LODGEPOLE PINE *(PINUS CONTORTA)*

Like ponderosa pine, lodgepole pine is found in both of the western forest regions. Since it ranges from the tidewater flats and bogs of the Pacific Ocean to 11,500-feet (3500 meters) elevation in the Rocky Mountains, it is not surprising that four recognized varieties exist. Perhaps the most common is the one found in the Rocky Mountains; it is illustrated in Figure 3–10.

Lodgepole is a medium-sized to small tree. Although its maximum size is recorded as 150 feet (45 meters) tall and 7 feet (2 meters) in diameter, heights of 70 feet (21 meters) are much more common. Growth of lodgepole pine is slow, and maturity is considered to be about 100 to 200 years, though trees more than 500 years old are recorded. From seedling to maturity, it is very intolerant of shade.

Lodgepole is a good example of the trees that are known as pioneer species. These trees are capable of rapidly regenerating areas that have been deforested by fire, flood, storm, or landslide. Lodgepole is well adapted to reseeding areas that have been badly burned.

Figure 3–10. Lodgepole pine. Note the narrow crown and the poor pruning of its lower, dead branches; both are typical of the inland form. Note also the clearcut block in the background. (Courtesy USDA Forest Service)

It begins producing seeds at a very early age, often when it is only 5 years old. Large seed crops are produced at frequent intervals. Lodgepole pine, however, has a high percentage of serotinous cones (serotinuous means "late"). These are cones that do not open each fall when the seeds are mature. The cones are sealed shut with resin and the seeds stored within them. These stored seeds remain viable for decades. Then there occurs the almost inevitable forest fire. The trees are killed and the forest floor is laid bare. The heat from the fire melts the sealing resin, the cones open, and thousands of seeds are released into the wind. A new forest arises from the ashes of the old. This new forest is very dense, having so many stems per acre that they all grow very tall and straight but do not become very large in diameter. These trees, known as poles, were used by local Indians to support their tepee lodges, hence the name lodgepole pine.

Aside from use by the Indians and for thousands of horse corrals throughout the early West, lodgepole was little utilized until recently. Lodgepole dimension timber is now shipped to all parts of the world.

The needles of lodgepole are about 2 inches (5 centimeters) long, in pairs, twisted and dark yellow-green. The cones are small, ¾ to 2 inches (1.91 to 5 cm) in length, and tan to brown in color. Scales near the base often are swollen and knob-like, while the whole cone often is sharply curved. The bark, on mountain trees, is thin, scaly, and brownish or gray in color.

3.9 DOUGLAS FIR (PSEUDOTSUGA MENZIESII)

Douglas fir is perhaps the single most important forest tree species in America today. About one half of the standing timber of the western forests is Douglas fir. More of it is harvested each year than any other American species, and it accounts for slightly less than 20 percent of all timber harvested each year. It occurs in both western forest regions. The inland form is found scattered from northern Canada down the Rocky Mountain chain into Mexico. The coastal form, which is perhaps the more important, is found west of the Sierra, Cascade, and Coastal ranges from California through British Columbia. Coastal Douglas fir is the largest tree in a land of large trees, the Pacific Northwest, and in the world it is second in size only to the fabulous redwoods of California. On good sites it can with time surpass 300 feet (91 meters) in height and 10 feet (3 meters) in diameter. It is a very long-lived species; specimens greater than 600 years old are not uncommon, and one with more than 1,375 growth rings has been reported.

Figure 3-11. Douglas fir on a small watershed in Washington. Notice how closely spaced these vigorous trees are. (Courtesy Weyerhaeuser Corp.)

A Douglas fir seedling requires light shade for best early survival and yet is less tolerant of shade than most of its common associates. Much like Eastern white pine, its initial growth is very slow. However, once rapid height growth has begun, it continues for many decades. Perhaps the most outstanding feature of Douglas fir is its ability to sustain this rapid growth in extremely dense stands. The result of so many large trees per acre is some of the heaviest volumes per acre found in any forest type anywhere in the world. This high density is shown in Figure 3-11 and Figure 2-10. At 100 years a good-quality stand can yield 170,000 board feet per acre. This is five or six times more than that found in the best stands of current eastern species.

The wood from Douglas fir is widely acclaimed as a dimension timber. Its large size has permitted the sawing not only of extremely wide and long boards but very massive structural timbers. It is, however, perhaps most widely known through Douglas fir plywood, a product in demand throughout the world. Perhaps it has only two shortcomings as the ideal timber producer: In very old stands it is often badly rotten in the center of the stem, and in young stands it does not prune its dead lower limbs and produce clear, knot-free lumber.

Like so many of our valuable timber species, Douglas fir is a subclimax type. This means that it invades a disturbed site and forms a dominant forest. Eventually, it gives way to the more tolerant species, such as western red cedar or western hemlock, which become established beneath it. This characteristic of Douglas fir, as with many other species, creates one of the forester's most troublesome problems, the perpetuation of a subclimax species.

In spite of its name, Douglas fir is not a fir. It is also sometimes known as Oregon pine, and it is not a pine. Its scientific name, *Pseudotsuga*, means false hemlock. It has some characteristics of all these genera, which created much confusion among early botanists. In spite of this, by its size alone, it is a very distinctive tree. The leaves are linear and blunt, rather than needlelike, and arise from all sides of the twig. The buds are sharp pointed, fusiform (shaped like a spindle), and covered with shiny brown scales. It is a very distinctive bud. The cones are light to dark brown and 3 to 4 inches (8 to 10 centimeters) long. Between each scale there emerges a three-lobed bract, brown and paperlike, which is a very distinctive characteristic. The bark on young trees is smooth, thin, grayish green, and often has small resin-filled blisters. On old stems the bark may be more than 1 foot (30.5 cm) thick, reddish brown, and deeply furrowed.

3.10 SITKA SPRUCE *(PICEA SITCHENSIS)*

Perhaps no tree is more characteristic of the coastal rain forest that extends from northern California to Alaska than Sitka spruce. It is found from tidewater flats to inland elevations of up to 2,000 feet (610 meters). It forms dense, pure, even-aged stands or grows in mixtures with Douglas fir and western hemlock. The tree itself is impressive, as it produces a very straight cylindrical stem that is often swollen or buttressed at the base. The branches of the crown are either ascending or horizontal, but the smaller branches tend to dangle straight down, giving the whole tree a characteristic ragged appearance.

Sitka spruce seed will germinate, as will that of western hemlock, wherever moisture is abundant, but the best survival and growth take place on mineral soil. Seedling development is slow, but once established growth is very rapid. This alone makes it distinct among our native spruces, which grow quite slowly. That it is intolerant of shade is also unique among our spruces. Sitka spruce 4 to 5 feet

(1 to 1.5 meters) in diameter and 200 feet (61 meters) tall are not uncommon in old growth stands. The largest ever recorded was 300 feet (91 meters) tall and 18 feet (6 meters) in diameter, which puts Sitka spruce in the same world of giants as Douglas fir and redwood. All these characteristics have made this species the target of many forest management activities.

The lumber produced from Sitka spruce is of exceptionally high quality. It is straight and even grained, and saws and seasons well. Of all our common native woods it is extremely strong for its weight. Because of this it was once widely used in the construction of aircraft frames. As late as World War II a very effective British bomber was built entirely of wood, mostly Sitka spruce. Today it is manufactured into both dimension and board lumber, and large volumes are made into pulp.

Its major enemies are the wind (it is very shallow rooted), fire, and a number of wood-rotting fungi.

Unlike most spruce species, Sitka spruce leaves are long (up to 1 inch or 2.5 cm), linear, flattened, and sharp pointed. They are shiny yellow-green on the upper surface and gray on the lower. The tan-colored cones may be from 2 to 4 inches (5 to 10 centimeters) long and are composed of thin papery scales. The tree bark is very distinctive in that it is composed of small, thin, loosely attached, silvery or purplish gray scales.

3.11 WESTERN HEMLOCK *(TSUGA HETEROPHYLLA)*

Western hemlock is one of the most characteristic and important species of the Pacific forest region. It extends from the north coast of California through western Oregon and Washington and then in a narrow strip along the coasts of Canada and Alaska. It also occurs inland in southeastern British Columbia and northern Idaho. It grows best between sea level and 2,000 feet (610 meters) in altitude along the coasts. This is the zone where the moist warm air from the Pacific Ocean moves inland to produce 70 or more inches (1800 mm) of rain a year. Even in these very productive sites its seedlings grow very slowly, often less than 2 inches (5 cm) in height per year. Once past the small sapling stage, however, the western hemlock grows quite rapidly, and at maturity it is a large tree often 4 feet (1.2 meters) in diameter and 200 feet (61 meters) tall. Few trees live beyond 500 years. It is an extremely shade tolerant tree, capable of developing and growing normally in an understory location. Its best growth rate, however, occurs when it receives full sunlight.

Western hemlock produces some seed each year and every 3 or 4 years produces a bumper crop. The seed will germinate wherever there is adequate moisture. In this wet forest its seedlings are often found developing normally on stumps, fallen logs, and moss-covered rocks. Because it is a very shallow rooted tree it is very susceptible to drought damage and to windthrow. It is also very sensitive to fire damage. The Indian paint fungus, a heart-rotting disease, and the hemlock looper, a caterpillar, can cause heavy damage.

When logging first began in this forest region, hemlock was almost ignored. Without much investigation it was assumed that the wood was similar to that of the familiar eastern hemlock, which is often brash (brittle) and weak. This is not the case, however, and today western hemlock is one of the most important timber species of the region. It is also the primary species used in the large sulfite pulp industry of the Northwest.

The leaves are linear, flattened in cross section, uniform in width from base to apex, and from ¼ to ¾ inch (.64 to 2 centimeters) long. The upper surface is a very glossy dark green. The leaves are spirally arranged around the twig, but each tiny petiole (leaf support) is twisted to one side or the other so that the leaves appear to be ranked or comblike. The cones are light brown, 1 inch (2.54 centimeters) or less in length, and have no prickles. The tree is easy to recognize from a distance due to a characteristically drooping central leader (terminal shoot) and the downward and then upward sweep of its branches, as shown in Figure 3–12.

3.12 PAPER BIRCH *(BETULA PAPYRIFERA)*

The range of paper birch is transcontinental. It stretches from Labrador in the east across all of Canada to central Alaska and extends northward nearly to the limits of tree growth. In the United States it occurs in the northern Rocky Mountains of Washington, Idaho, and Montana, in the Lakes States, in New England, and in scattered localities down the Appalachian Ridge to North Carolina. It is truly a tree of the northern forest and seldom grows naturally where the average July temperature exceeds 70°F (21°C).

It is a shade-intolerant species and usually is found scattered in the mixed forest of the Northeast. Like its associate, aspen, it is a very successful pioneer species and, following a fire in the north woods, its light buoyant seed can quickly colonize the burned-out forest. Pure even-aged stands of paper birch are formed. Beneath the birch there slowly develop the more shade-tolerant, slower growing spruce and fir trees. See Figure 3–13.

Figure 3-12. (*Left*) A young, open grown western hemlock in Idaho. Notice the characteristic sweep of the branches. (Courtesy USDA Forest Service)

Figure 3-13. (*Right*) Paper birch trees in Wisconsin. The twin trees are likely to be of sprout origin. (Courtesy USDA Forest Service)

Paper birch seedlings are very weak and tender and grow very slowly for the first year. Once established, growth is rapid for about 30 years, after which it slows. Mature trees average about 60 feet (18 meters) in height and 10 to 15 inches (25 to 38 centimeters) in diameter, although the record size is 120 feet (37 meters) tall and 6 feet (1.8 meters) in diameter. It is a short-lived tree and rarely exceeds 120 years of age.

The bark of paper birch was peeled from the stem by the northern Indians and used in the manufacture of many items. The beautiful and brilliantly engineered birch-bark canoe is the most well-known product, but the bark was also used to cover wigwams and to make a wide variety of baskets and buckets, some of which were employed as cooking utensils. Even today many novelty items are made from birch bark. The hard, dense wood is highly valued for the manufacture of dowels, pegs, spools, and small specialty items.

Aside from fire, which often creates a new birch forest, there are relatively few natural enemies of white birch. Post-logging decadence and birch dieback are environmental diseases associated with heating and drying of the forest floor.

Paper birch is easily recognized by its bark. Though it is dark brown at first, it soon develops the characteristic white or creamy color and begins to split and separate into paperlike strips. The 2- to 3-inch (5 to 8 centimeters) long oval leaves are dark green above and yellow-green below. The margin of each leaf has a number of large sawteeth each of which has smaller sawteeth. The brownish twigs have small buds that are covered with dark brown, gummy scales. There are a number of paper-barked birches used as ornamentals. Perhaps the most common of these is the European white birch, *Betula alba*.

3.13 SUGAR MAPLE *(ACER SACCHARUM)*

Sugar maple is common to both the northern and central forests, and is one of the most useful and beloved trees of both regions. Its hard, strong, smooth-grained wood is a favorite of the furniture industry and is used as flooring, particularly in gymnasiums, in hardwood plywood, and in specialty products such as bowling pins. It is the source of maple syrup and maple sugar from the northern forest and as such is the the basis of a thriving industry. Small holes are drilled into the wood of the tree, and each is fitted with a small pipe. In the early spring as the tree breaks winter dormancy, sap pours from these pipes into buckets or plastic tubing that leads to collection points in the forest. The sap is then thickened by evaporation over heat to become maple syrup. Continued evaporation results in light-tan maple sugar. Sugar maple trees also supply browse food, particularly for deer. This is a favorite tree for ornamental and street planting, even well beyond its natural range. Finally, and perhaps quite importantly, the blaze of fall color provided by its foliage is an annual source of great delight to all who are so fortunate as to view it.

Throughout its range, sugar maple is found on a great variety of sites, but its best development occurs on moist but well-aerated soils. Even at best the growth of sugar maple is very slow. At maturity, which is from 300 to 400 years, it may be 70 to 100 feet (21 to 31 meters) tall and 2 to 3 feet (61 to 91 centimeters) in diameter. See Figure 3–14.

Figure 3–14. An old growth sugar maple in a northern forest of mixed hardwoods and conifers. (Courtesy USDA Forest Service)

Maple is one of the most shade tolerant of all our major hardwood trees. It can produce, at maturity, vast quantities of seed. Consequently, a dense almost carpetlike maple seedling understory is a common feature of the maple "flats" of the north woods. Like most tolerant trees, it is able to respond to release after decades of suppression.

The leaves of sugar maple are 3 to 5 inches (8 to 13 centimeters) in diameter, five lobed, and palmately formed (shaped like an open hand). The margins of the lobes are smooth, not sawtoothed as in elm or red maple. The leaves are opposite, that is, they occur in pairs upon the lustrous brown twigs. The 1-inch (2.5 cm) long winged seed is very distinctive. These occur in pairs joined at the seed so that the wings extend oppositely to each other. The bark is variable in that it may be furrowed, scaly, or in between. It is always gray.

3.14 YELLOW POPLAR *(LIRIODENDRON TULIPIFERA)*

One of the most distinctive trees of the eastern United States, the yellow poplar, often called "tulip tree," actually is not a poplar. It is a member of the magnolia family. Yellow poplar is a beautiful tree with large tuliplike flowers (hence the name tulip tree) and four-lobed leaves on long leaf attachments (*petioles*). The flower, varying from yellow-green to cream, does not appear until well after the leaves develop.

Yellow poplar is also one of our most important timber producers. It is one of the largest eastern hardwoods, attaining heights of 80 to 150 feet (35 to 45 meters) and diameters of 4 to 6 feet (1.2 to 1.8 meters). These characteristics are pictured in Figure 3-15. The trunks of mature trees support pyramidal crowns and have ridged and furrowed gray-brown bark. The root system is deep and wide spreading. The tree grows well on moist, well-drained, loose-textured soils of moderate depth. Yellow poplar is shade intolerant; on good sites, however, growth is so rapid that young trees may overtake their competition. Yellow poplar occurs in mixture with gum, oak, red maple, loblolly pine, and many other species.

Figure 3-15. Yellow poplar. (Courtesy USDA Forest Service)

The wood of yellow poplar is soft and easy to work and is extensively used for veneer and pulpwood. Products made from its wood are furniture, pallets, crates, baskets, and boxes. Over one half of the U.S. supply of yellow poplar wood comes from the southeastern states, although its range extends from central Michigan east to the Atlantic Ocean and south to the Gulf of Mexico.

3.15 SWEETGUM *(LIQUIDAMBAR STYRACIFLUA)*

Sweetgum, also called redgum, is found from Connecticut southward throughout the East to central Florida and eastern Texas. It grows as far west as Mississippi, Arkansas, and Oklahoma, and north to southern Illinois. It is also found in scattered locations other than those mentioned. Even though sweetgum is a typical southern bottomland, shade-intolerant species that grows in damp soil along rivers and streams, it also grows on hills.

It is easy to recognize because it has distinctive star-shaped leaves and conspicuous fruit, the "gum balls" pictured in Figure 3–16. The leaves are 5 to 7 inches (13 to 18 cm) wide and have five to seven pointed lobes with toothed margins. The leaves are bright green, turning red and gold in the fall. The "gum balls" hang by a stem and have

Figure 3–16. Sweetgum leaves and gum ball fruit. (Courtesy USDA Forest Service)

sharp thornlike points. Corky wings or ridges along the twigs also help identify the tree. The heartwood or center of the older tree is brownish red, hence the name redgum.

Sweetgum trees grow 80 to 120 feet (24 to 36 meters) tall and attain a diameter of 3 to 5 feet (60 to 150 centimeters). The bark is gray to brown, ridged, and furrowed. The wood of sweetgum is valuable for veneer, lumber, and pulpwood. The lumber from sweetgum is employed for interior trim in houses and other buildings and also for furniture. Railroad crossties, shipping pallets, crates, and boxes are also made from the poorer-quality lumber of sweetgum. The "gum" for which it is named exudes from wounds in the bark. It is used locally as a natural chewing gum or may be collected and used as a flavoring or perfume.

3.16 WHITE OAK *(QUERCUS ALBA)*

The oak family with its many species is our most important genus of hardwoods. There are two broad groups of oaks on the American continent: white oak and red oak. There are about 70 species of oak and over half of these grow in the South. More native timber is furnished by oak annually in the United States than any other group of broad-leaved trees. Some examples of the white oak group are white oak (*Quercus alba*), over-cup oak (*Quercus lyrata*), and post oak (*Quercus stellata*).

White oak is the most significant species of the white oak group and it furnishes nearly three fourths of the lumber marketed as white oak. The leaves are deciduous (all are shed annually), 5 to 9 inches (13 to 23 centimeters) long, and 2 to 4 inches (5 to 10 centimeters) wide. They have seven to nine lobes, which are rounded and divided by narrow sinuses varying in depth and often extending nearly to the midrib of the leaf. Acorns from ½ to ¾ inch (1.3 to 1.9 cm) in length, set in a bowllike cup covered with wartlike scales, are produced and fall each year. They germinate in the fall.

The white oak is a large tree 80 to 100 feet (24 to 30 meters) in height and 3 to 4 feet (90 to 120 centimeters) in diameter. In the open this tree is characterized by a wide-spreading crown, as seen in Figures 3–17 and 3–1. Under forest conditions the white oak grows a straight trunk that supports a small crown. The bark of this tree is in narrow, vertical ridges, and often, gray scaly plates.

White oak develops a deep root system and is found on many types of soil, such as sandy plains, rich uplands, gravelly ridges, well-drained second bottoms, and coves. It develops best on deep, well-

Figure 3-17. White oak on the Mount Vernon estate in Virginia. (Courtesy USDA Forest Service)

drained soils. Growth usually is good except on very dry and shallow soils. White oak is found in association with other upland oaks, white ash, sweetgum, yellow poplar, blackgum, hickory, black cherry, American beech, shortleaf pine, eastern white pine, loblolly pine, and eastern hemlock. Although rare in Florida, it is native to all states east of Kansas and Nebraska.

The wood of white oak is used for lumber, pulp, furniture, barrels, railroad crossties, and fuel.

3.17 ASPEN *(POPULUS TREMULOIDES)*

The aspen is a tree of moist, cool climates. As such it has the widest range of any tree in North America. Found in the northern Rocky Mountain, Alaskan, and Pacific Northwest forests, it spreads from Maine to western Alaska and, at high elevations, south through the Rocky Mountains into Mexico. Throughout this great area it is found on a large variety of soils. Perhaps its best development is found in the northern Lakes States.

Aspen usually is a small tree, about 70 feet (21 meters) tall and 1 foot (30.48 centimeters) in diameter, although occasional trees may be twice this size. Its growth is rapid and it is short lived. It is an excellent example of a pioneer species. It produces an abundance of seed, starting at an early age. The seed is very light and can be carried by the wind for long distances. The seed requires moist mineral soil in order to sprout, and the seedling is very intolerant of shade. Consequently, most of the seed produced either never sprouts or is soon killed by competing vegetation or by brief dry spells. However, should the drifting seed find a deforested area, such as that produced by an intense wildfire, aspen will quickly colonize the entire area.

Once established it is preyed upon by a large number of insects and diseases. Its bark is eagerly eaten by a number of rodents, and its twigs are a favorite browse for deer and moose. In spite of this, once established aspen tends to remain for long periods rather than give way to more tolerant longer-lived species. The major reason for this is its ability to produce root suckers. Should the top be removed by cutting, by a fire, or by being girdled by beavers, a number of new trees will emerge from the roots and maintain the existence of the tree. This characteristic, though present in other species, is especially strong in aspen. It is the basis of much of the forest management of this species.

The tree is easy to identify. The small almost circular leaves have small wavy teeth along their margins. The leaf stalks (*petioles*) are long and flattened. This condition causes the leaves to flutter in even gentle breezes, hence the name quaking or trembling aspen. The twigs are shiny reddish brown, and the scaly winter buds are the same color, large, and sharp pointed. The smooth creamy or greenish white bark is its most distinctive characteristic. See Figure 3–18.

3.18 NORTHERN RED OAK *(QUERCUS RUBRA)*

The name of this species is a little misleading because northern red oak occurs in the northern, central, and southern forest regions, from Maine to Minnesota, to eastern Oklahoma, to southern Alabama, to coastal Virginia; it is second only to eastern white oak in the extent of its range. Nevertheless, it is perhaps more common in the northern part of its range than white oak. Its wood is put to a large number of uses, ranging from fine furniture to pulpwood.

It is found on a wide variety of sites, ranging from dry rocky soils to deep alluvial stream side soils. It perhaps grows best on the deep, fresh soils of north-facing lower slopes of mountain coves. On such sites it can grow at an average rate of diameter growth of 2.5 inches (6 centimeters) per 10 years, which is much faster than the more generally valuable white oak. On the average it will reach a

Figure 3-18. Young aspen being harvested by a hydraulic tree shear. (Courtesy Caterpillar Tractor)

mature size of 70 to 80 feet (21 to 24 meters) in height and 2 to 3 feet (61 to 91 centimeters) in diameter. Some individuals will become twice this size.

Because of its rapid growth, good form, and generally high value, northern red oak is the oak most generally favored by foresters throughout most of its range. It is not without problems. Like most of the oaks, it may produce an abundance of acorns on a regular cycle, but very few of them result in seedlings, for acorns are an important food for a large number of animals. In a given year nearly the whole crop of acorns can be consumed. In other years weevils may destroy most of the acorn crop. Once established, however, the seedlings have the ability to grow rapidly, and, as with most oaks, if the top of the seedling is destroyed, it can sprout back quickly from dormant buds at the base of the stem. The northern red oak is attacked by a number of insects and diseases, of which perhaps the worst is oak wilt, which usually is fatal. It is rated as intermediate in shade tolerance, but is generally less tolerant than its associates, which is also a deterrent to its effective regeneration.

The leaves are 5 to 8 inches (13 to 20 centimeters) in length and have 7 to 11 bristle-tipped lobes. Both surfaces are smooth and have little or none of the soft hairs, known as pubescence, on the leaves or stems of other species. Red oak acorns are variable in size; some are as much as 1 inch (2.54 centimeters) long, subglobose in shape (not or nearly global), and fitted into very shallow saucer-like cups. The bark on young stems is grayish green and smooth. On mature stems the bark is nearly black and has long wide ridges separated by narrow fissures (cracks or openings).

3.19 SUMMARY

Many trees have a typical crown and stem shape when grown in the open without competition from other trees. In a forest this form usually is modified to a longer straight stem and narrow crown. Tree age also influences the general form of a tree.

Tree species may be identified by the color, shape, size, and texture of their twigs, buds, leaves, flowers, fruit, and bark.

Each species of tree has an accepted common name, such as paper birch, red oak, or shortleaf pine. Many trees have a number of common names, particularly when they have a very wide range. This can create confusion, which is overcome by the use of scientific names. Each tree has only one accepted and official scientific name, which consists of a generic or genus name and a specific or species name. These names are in Latin because it is a fixed language that no longer is subject to change. The generic name starts with a capital letter; the specific name always starts with a lowercase letter.

There are two main groups of trees: conifers (softwood) and broadleaf (hardwood). Conifers have needle- or scalelike leaves and bear seeds in cones. With two exceptions all conifers are evergreens. Most North American broadleaf species are deciduous, that is, shed their leaves in the fall.

chapter 4

Tree and Forest Terminology

4.1 TREES INTEREST PEOPLE

Trees have always been of great interest to humans, possibly because they served as homes for the earliest people. During the course of history, the tree has been honored in verse and song, such as in Joyce Kilmer's poem "Trees" and in the popular wartime hit "Don't Sit under the Apple Tree." Leprechauns and wood sprites have been imagined to live in the forest glade, perpetuating stories and superstitions in the "old country" and here in the United States as well. Winds rushing through treetops have sounded to men like melodies of the legendary creatures of the primeval forest.

Human interest in trees can be attributed to many factors. One could be the fact that some trees, the deciduous types, bare their branches during the winter and seem to be dead, but with the beginning of spring sprout little buds of green, proving that truly there is eternal life in the forest.

4.2 THE ANATOMY OF A TREE

Trees are single-stemmed woody plants that have roots well anchored in the ground and that, for the most part, grow upright. The main

53

stem is called a *bole* or trunk. The bole supports branches and leaves, referred to as the *crown,* and transports minerals and water from the soil.

Trees usually start from seeds. The evergreens, for example pines, have cones from which naked, nutlike, winged seeds fall. The cottonwood and other poplars have very tiny seeds with fine silky hairs that become airborne and often land many miles from the parent tree. Birds and mammals may transport seeds great distances, carrying such fruits as pits from cherries, beans from the locust; nuts like the soft-shelled acorns, fleshy, winged seeds of maples, and hard-shelled hickory nuts and walnuts. These carriers plus the winds and floodwaters help account for the widespread distribution of most species.

The tiny, frail seedlings push up from the ground's surface and often are attacked by animals and birds that pick at them for food. Hardwood seedlings require about 3 or 4 weeks to become miniature trees. Trees may also *regenerate* by sprouting from roots or from stumps. Another type of tree propagation is *layering,* the rooting of an undetached branch lying on or partially buried in the soil. Such a branch is capable of independent growth, and eventually is separated from the original plant.

The underground part of a forest is made up of the roots of trees, shrubs, and *herbaceous* plants, those having little or no woody tissue and usually single-seasoned. Roots of trees are seldom dug up except where land is being reclaimed for agricultural or construction purposes, where the roots are to be used for medicinal or artistic purposes, or where, especially in the southeastern United States, residual stumps and taproots of old-growth longleaf and slash pines are used to make turpentine, rosin, and various pine oils.

The root system of a tree may consist of four parts: (1) a *taproot,* which when present anchors the tree firmly in the ground and supplies the main support for the tree; (2) *lateral roots,* which usually extend beyond the crown spread and help keep the tree in an upright position; (3) *fibrous roots,* a mass of fine roots most found in the upper soil; and (4) thin-walled *root hairs,* which grow from the smaller fibrous roots and absorb water and minerals. These may live only a few days.

Because root hairs die off after a few days, trees are always growing new ones to reach more soil. Many trees also depend upon *mycorrhizae,* a fungus which grows on or within roots that acts in the same manner as the root hairs. Mycorrhizae form a sheath around the roots, enabling fingerlike *mycelia* to grow and extend into the soil, thus allowing the tree to absorb moisture and mineral food.

If you cut through a tree, across the bole or a branch, you may see light- and dark-colored *rings*. The light rings are produced from fast growth in the spring and the dark ones from slow growth in the summer. These serve to reveal the age of the tree, since a light and dark ring together constitute a year's growth. To determine the age, one may count either light or dark rings. It is easier to count the dark ones because they are more conspicuous.

A tree increases its diameter by producing new cells just under the bark. Growth takes place just beneath the bark. Rings that are 1 year or more old keep the same size they had when they were produced. It follows that what goes on just below the bark is vitally important. The often darker-colored interior wood near the tree's center is called *heartwood* and is no longer living.

The outer part of a tree trunk, that outside the most-recent annual ring, is made up of four sections or layers, as follows: the outer bark, which protects the tree from radical changes in temperature, injuries, diseases, insects, and drying; the inner bark, called *phloem,* which translocates sugars made in the leaves to the branches, trunk, and roots, where it is converted into vital growth substances; the *cambium,* a layer of cells where the growth that produces the annual ring and the phloem takes place; and the sapwood, called *xylem,* which transports a mixture of mineral nutrients, water, and other substances called *sap* to the leaves.

The cambium increases the size of the trunk by making a layer of new wood each year. Its outer cells form phloem, while its inner cells form xylem, which is wood. Bark is produced by special cambial cells and by old non-living phloem cells. Xylem cells made in the spring are large and thin walled; those made in the summer are smaller, thick walled, and darker in color. As indicated previously, spring and summer growth taken together make an annual ring. The heartwood, the major function of which is mechanical, gives strength and stiffness to the tree trunk.

4.3 TREES ARE CHEMICAL MACHINES

A tree uses solar energy to manufacture wood fiber. Nature supplies the tree with carbon dioxide from the air, nutrients and water from the ground, and light energy from the sun, and the tree, a remarkable factory, combines them. It captures a lot of energy as it grows and stores it, as discussed in Section 7.5.

The four most essential factors in tree life are *water* (the chemical elements hydrogen and oxygen combined as H_2O molecules); *nutrients* (elements such as nitrogen, phosphorus, sulfur, potassium, iron, manganese, zinc, boron, calcium, magnesium, and molybdenum); *foods* (such as glucose, a form of sugar consisting of carbon, hydrogen, and oxygen combined as $C_6H_{12}O_6$ molecules); and *light* (from the sun or an artificial source).

Photosynthesis is the process of producing glucose, a plant food, from water and carbon dioxide by the use of light energy, with gaseous oxygen as a by-product. The glucose is energy-rich. The following chemical equation represents the process of photosynthesis in simplified form:

$$\text{Energy} + 6\,CO_2 + 6\,H_2O \rightarrow C_6H_{12}O_6 + 6\,O_2 \uparrow$$

Note that this equation is "balanced" as each side has the same number of C, O, and H atoms; atoms are neither made nor destroyed, they are simply put into new combinations. The equation says that one molecule of glucose and six of oxygen in gaseous form are made from six molecules of carbon dioxide and six of water.

Photosynthesis takes place in the tree leaves. They contain small food-producing bodies called *chloroplasts,* which contain *chlorophyll,* a substance that gives green color to the leaves. Sunlight enters through the leaf's surface and CO_2 enters through millions of minute openings in the leaf called *stomata* (see Figure 4-1). Water and nutrients reach the chlorophyll via the xylem. The

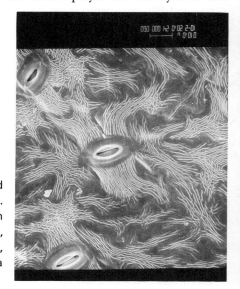

Figure 4-1. Stomata on a hydrangea leaf, magnified 1,000 times by an electron microscope. They allow exchange of oxygen and carbon dioxide. (Courtesy of Dr. James W. Hardin, Professor and Curator of the Herbarium, Department of Botany, North Carolina State University.)

stomata usually are open in the presence of sunlight and are closed during darkness. When oxygen is being generated, it leaves through the stomata and enters the atmosphere.

The glucose created by photosynthesis is a plant food. For it to be used as a food, some of its molecules must be broken down in the process called *respiration,* promoted by appropriate *enzymes.* The basic chemical equation for respiration is

$$C_6H_{12}O_6 + 6\,O_2 \rightarrow 6\,H_2O + 6\,CO_2 \uparrow + energy$$

Each molecule of glucose is combined with six of oxygen taken from the air in the leaves. This process produces six molecules of water, six of carbon dioxide, and released energy. The carbon dioxide enters the atmosphere. The sum of the processes of building up and breaking down substances containing carbon is called *metabolism.*

A small part of the released energy appears as heat, which very slightly warms the leaf, but most of it is used chemically to produce or enlarge growth cells, arriving at the cells via the cambium layer. The fibrous substance produced, composed of carbon, hydrogen, and oxygen, called *cellulose,* is high in energy content but has a molecular composition different from that of glucose; it makes up about 60 percent of the tree.

Water is a necessity if a tree is to grow and thrive. It dissolves soil minerals and transports them to the leaves as nutrients. It is a source of hydrogen in photosynthesis. Water is also necessary to build up the growing cells and thus make the tree rigid. Oxygen in the soil is also of strategic importance to support respiratory metabolism in the tree root. Where the concentration of oxygen is too low, such as in nonporous soils or in areas where the soil is waterlogged, or beneath city pavement plant growth ceases and death may occur. However, some plants common to waterlogged swamp soils have evolved structures that are believed to acquire oxygen directly from the atmosphere. For example, the root projections of cypress trees, commonly referred to as "knees," extend above the water, perhaps making gas exchange with the atmosphere possible.

Respiration takes place 24 hours a day, whereas photosynthesis needs sunlight and ceases during the night. However, photosynthesis proceeds at about ten times the rate of respiration. This cycle results in several net effects: (1) All the carbon atoms that enter the photosynthesis reaction go into glucose, but not all of the oxygen atoms are emitted (as a gas) by the tree during daylight; (2) at all times, carbon dioxide is emitted into the atmosphere from respiration; (3) in the daytime, the oxygen emission resulting from photosynthesis greatly outclasses the carbon dioxide emission from respiration. The concentration of carbon dioxide in the atmosphere of the earth stays at about 0.03 percent, while oxygen, maintained by the combined effect of all the green plants of the earth and sea, comprises nearly 20 percent of the atmosphere.

In relatively recent years the word *biomass* was adopted as a name or label for "substance, weighable material, that exists as a result of biological production and growth from more primary materials," or, more narrowly, the material substance produced in a forest. Thus, in forestry, biomass can be thought of as "accumulated and stored energy in the form of organic material." It follows that in many more intensive forms of commercial forestry the objective is to produce biomass as quickly as possible, at the least cost, per unit of biomass produced on the least possible land area. This is particularly true in pulpwood or energywood (firewood) production, but not necessarily in the production of lumber, poles, piling, veneer, and the like.

Biomass production per year per acre is a function of many factors. Obviously, it must depend upon the availability of moisture, sunlight, and nutrients in the soil. It will also depend upon the tree species and their spacing and age. As trees grow, the root system enlarges, and this can result in more rapid uptake of minerals and water. Enlargement of the forest canopy can alter the environment near the ground and the microclimate. It follows that modern research in forest biomass production is far from simple and requires much technology and many measurements.

The organized living tissue of a tree, called *protoplasm,* contains from 75 to 90 percent water. Soft fruits such as peaches and apples are 85 percent water. Water present in a tree is released as vapor through the stomata of the leaves; this process is called *transpiration.* During this water loss the leaves open their stomata and at the same time admit carbon dioxide. The more transpiration that takes place, the greater is the need for water in the soil around the tree roots.

Many interesting theories about the mechanism of transpiration have been offered, but none has been scientifically accepted as the method by which water is raised from the roots and up the trunk to the leaves. A popular theory is based upon molecular cohesion and the action of pulling on the end of a chain, in which each link pulls upon the one next to it. Similarly, the water molecules leaving the stomata are thought to pull upon those below them, with the stress extending through the water molecules in the xylem, resulting in an upward pull on the water molecules in the roots and soil.

Hot summer days produce a greater amount of transpiration because dry summer winds speed up the transpiration process, making the tree thirsty, so to speak. If the amount of water transpired is greater than that available from the soil, the cells around the stomata, called guard cells, become soft and the stomata close. This causes the intake of carbon dioxide to stop, photosynthesis ceases, and the tree stops growing. While the movement of water in trees is mainly upward from roots to leaves, there is some conduction of water and sap radially outward in the trunk.

4.4 TREE SIZE AND TYPE CLASSIFICATIONS

Tree age and size can be described in a general and approximate way by use of such words as seedling, sapling, pole-size, mature, and veteran. A stand of trees can be even-aged or all-aged. A forest made up principally of one species is a *pure* stand, while one composed of several species is a *mixed* stand.

Trees are also classified by the positions of their crowns relative to the general level of the forest *canopy*, the covering created by the crowns interweaving with each other:

Dominant: A tree having a well-developed crown that extends above the general level of the other crowns and is exposed to full light from above and partial light from the sides.

Codominant: A tree with smaller crown than the dominants that helps form the general level of the forest canopy and receives full light from above but limited amount from the sides.

Intermediate: A small-crowned tree crowded into the general level of the forest canopy, receiving some light from above and virtually none from the sides.

Suppressed: A tree with poorly developed crown, beneath the level of the canopy (overtopped), receiving very little light from above or the sides.

Foresters refer to a measure of the number and size of trees in a given area as *stand density*. It indicates whether the forest is under stocked, medium stocked, or well stocked. For example, if the canopy of a tract of timber is closed over as much as 40 to 70 percent, it is medium stocked.

4.5 THE SUBDIVISIONS OF FORESTRY

As stated earlier, only recently has forestry become a subject of scientific study. Around the 1910s the first experimental stations were established and research began.

The practice of forestry requires consideration of all the natural elements, such as air, earth, fire, water, animals, and plants, plus the needs of people. Study of the requirements for plant growth, management of the soil, schedules for felling of trees, use of wood and slash, and preparations for new crops are all very important aspects of *forest management,* which can be broken down into specific divisions as follows:

Dendrology. In its broadest sense this is the study of trees. In forestry education it is restricted to tree identification and information on where the various types grow. Obviously, one interested in forestry begins his or her education with this subject.

Silvics. This includes the biotic (living) and abiotic (nonliving) factors that influence tree growth. Silvics covers a multitude of topics ranging from the influence of bacteria and rabbits (biotic) to rainfall, wind, and soil depth (abiotic). Silvics is the groundwork for the practice of silviculture.

Forest Soils. The chemical, physical, and biological characteristics of soil influence the growth of trees. In the establishment, management, and use of a forest, knowledge of soil factors is important and essential. Search for a better understanding of how these factors influence tree growth has resulted in the establishment of a great amount of scientific knowledge about forest soils.

Silviculture. This is forest cultivation, the growing and tending of forest trees, employing the scientific knowledge that constitutes silvics, aimed at producing maximum yields of valuable crops and services. Forest managers must know the soil characteristics and capabilities in an area to be planted, the water drainage, and whether trees can reproduce there. They must protect newly planted trees from natural and mechanical injury.

Mensuration. This is the measurement of the volume and growth of logs, single trees, and timbered areas. This science is concerned with the measurement of existing forest land, forest yield, and production.

Protection. Animals, fire, diseases, wind, and insects can seriously damage a forest if it is not protected. Study of the behavior of these enemies of the forest and knowledge of how to develop strategies to counter-act and control them is called forest protection.

Wood Technology. What the various kinds of wood are made up of chemically, their physical properties, their behavior under variable conditions such as of humidity and temperature, and what they can be used for come under the heading of wood technology. Wood technologists and utilization experts work closely with each other because their fields overlap and interact in many respects.

Utilization. Some of the trees in a forest will eventually be used to satisfy various human needs, such as for buildings, furniture, paper, containers, and pallets. Forest managers need to know what use to make of existing trees and what kinds of trees to grow for desired uses.

Valuation. Forestry constitutes a business, and like other businessess it must be run in an orderly manner. When a store owner has goods to sell, he must set a price based on costs, overhead, and the like, and not on "guesstimation." So it is with a forest. Whether for private or public use, the forest has value, and each tree in it has a value depending on species, size and age, and consumer need.

Regulation. This is the keeping of tree inventories, and also involves the principles of where, how, and if they should be harvested for the definite economic, environmental and esthetic goals.

Administration. Every business must have people who are in charge of the whole operation. Forest administration is the carrying out of policies and the guidance of procedures. It includes handling the personnel problems of forestry, such as the selection of workers, their schooling, and the assignment of priorities for personnel and funds.

Policy Setting. Business and government both need to have people who consider the possible consequences of various possible actions and assess the amount of good or harm that may come from them, so as to determine the nature of the policies that should be followed and carried out through suitable rules and regulations, laws, and ordinances. This function could be called the determination of desirable strategies and actions in forestry.

Other specialists who come into contact with those who study and manage forests are in the areas of economics, zoology, pathology, finance, engineering, and public administration. Other fields of study and control could be listed in this connection. Usually, management of public parks and tree preservation therein is not regarded as an aspect of forest management.

4.6 SUMMARY

Trees, one of the types of green plants, have always been close to the lives of humans. The major components of a tree are root system, bole, branches, and leaves. Tree age may be determined by counting annual rings.

In the leaves, through photosynthesis, nutrients and water from the soil and carbon dioxide from the air are converted into plant food, glucose, which is an energy-rich carbohydrate, and oxygen, which is emitted into the atmosphere. Then, under the bark of the trunk and the branches, the glucose is converted into cellulose, a woody substance. This process of food digestion followed by manufacture of body substance is an example of metabolism. The taking in and emission of gases and vapor as a result of energy transfer is called respiration (i.e., breathing), while transpiration is the passage of water vapor through a leaf surface.

Material substance created by tree growth is today often referred to as biomass and is a form of stored energy. Therefore, biomass production is today one of the ways being considered to use solar energy in place of the dwindling world oil supply.

Trees are classified into species, and also by age, size, and relative stature in the forest stand.

Forestry can be divided into a number of subdivisions: dendrology, silvics, forest soils, silviculture, mensuration, protection, wood technology, utilization, valuation, regulation, administration, and policy setting.

chapter 5
Forests and the Environment

5.1 THE SCIENCE KNOWN AS ECOLOGY

For a long time people have realized that living things are greatly
affected by other living things and by their surroundings, their
environment, and that organisms also tend to affect their surroundings. In the present century, such interrelationships have been studied
very seriously, and that study has developed a division of science
called *ecology*. The science of ecology as a whole is concerned
with the interrelationships of organisms and their physical environments and with other organisms. The word ecology is also applied
to a specific organism, for example, the "ecology" of loblolly pine,
which refers to all the relations between that species and other
organisms and its environment.

Our study of forestry will include the ecology of various organisms. An example is the ecology of forest game, where hunting is
utilized to forestall animal overpopulation, thus preventing overbrowsing and wintertime starvation. This may be compared with the
study of human ecology, which is very important because of the
prospect of world overpopulation and worldwide insufficiency of
food and energy. Human activities affect the natural world; a simple

63

example is that sewage can kill fish. As the population continues to grow and material productivity increases, the impact of human activities will become progressively greater. People cannot live apart from the natural world because they rely on it for food, materials for shelter and clothing, and recreation. Thus human survival depends on maintaining the natural world in a state of vigor and productivity.

One of the most visible examples of a vigorous productive environment is the forest. So we will discuss the basics of forest ecology. Forest ecology is a growing science with new knowledge coming both from research and from the results of forest management experiences. The stockpile of accumulated ecological knowledge is often tapped by foresters and legislators for methods and ways to improve our environment.

5.2 THE BASICS OF FOREST ECOLOGY

Tree leaves employ the energy of sunlight to convert carbon dioxide from the air and water and minerals from the soil into woody material. Tree leaves also collect dust, which is washed off by rain and falls to the ground, where some of the dust particles enter and become part of the soil. Runoff water from a forest carries some of the dust particles into streams, where part of it may be consumed by organisms, including fish. If the dust happens to have come from an industrial plant manufacturing a poison, it could harm the fish or a person who eats the fish.

For a tree to live, it must have water. The availability of water depends upon the amount of precipitation, the nature of the soil, and the level of the water table (the upper limit of the ground wholly saturated with water, as indicated by the level at which water naturally stands in a well). The water table fluctuates with precipitation and surface use.

Some forests (evergreen) are not noticeably affected by seasonal changes in the weather; others (deciduous) are drastically affected, losing all their leaves each autumn. The growth rate of forest trees depends upon a number of factors, mainly amount of sunlight, type of soil, availability of water, temperature, and the genetic potential of the trees. Most of these factors are related to climate, directly or indirectly.

5.3 OUR CLIMATE AND THE FORESTS

Air temperature within a forest during the summer usually is 6 to 8° Fahrenheit (3 to 4°C) below that outside the forest, but in the winter the temperature of a forest is very close to that of open areas or sometimes warmer by a few degrees. Soil temperature in the open on a summer day may reach 90°F (32°C), while soil temperature in an adjacent forest stand is 20°F (11°C) lower. In a coniferous forest it takes longer for the forest soil to freeze in winter, but it also takes longer for ground thaw to take place in the spring, because of the insulating effect of the canopy and the ground litter on the forest floor.

The word "climate" refers to the weather conditions that prevail or exist at a particular place over a period of years, with respect to air temperature, humidity, wind speeds, amount of rain and snow, and the like, in terms both of averages and of high and low extremes. The climate of a region affects whether or not there will be a forest and what type of forest if there is one; but the presence or absence of a large amount of forested land may also have some effect upon the weather and, therefore, upon the climate.

A forest modifies climate by obstructing and detouring the path of wind and dissipating it to a marked degree. Under normal conditions the wind velocity in a forest is considerably less than that in the open. Windbreaks and shelterbelts have demonstrated the effect forests can have in reducing wind speed. A shelterbelt or protective belt is a strip of trees and/or shrubs maintained primarily to provide shelter from wind, sun, snowdrift, and the like. In the United States the phrase shelterbelt refers mainly to belts that protect fields; those protecting farmsteads are termed windbreaks.[1]

The presence or absence of trees can influence soil erosion to a great extent. In Oklahoma and Kansas, in the 1930s, there was a large region of the Great Plains consisting of rich farmland that was heavily cultivated. Then a prolonged period of little rainfall and heavy winds stripped the entire region of much of its topsoil, leaving behind a vast desert-like area called the Dust Bowl. The effect of this tragedy might have been less if landowners had increased the proportion of the land given over to trees and other permanent vegetation.

Cottonwoods or other rapid-growing shade-intolerant trees that retain but few lower branches are most often used in windbreak canopies for the benefit of their peak crowns, while shorter trees are planted along the sides of the peak trees. The edges of the windbreak are then planted with shrubbery. On the leeward side of a windbreak the wind is reduced for a distance 40 times the height of the trees and for a much smaller distance on the windward side. Evaporation from the soil, transpiration of vegetation, potential

---

[1] F.C. Ford-Robinson, ed., *Terminology of Forest Science, Technology, Practice and Products* (Washington, D.C.: Society of American Foresters, 1971), p 237.

Figure 5-1. Shelterbelt of loblolly pines 8 years after planting on a Hoke County, North Carolina farm. (Courtesy U.S. Soil Conservation Service)

Figure 5-2. Farm homestead windbreak consisting of loblolly pines and ligustrum, on a Washington County, North Carolina farm. (Courtesy U.S. Soil Conservation Service)

damage from snowdrifts, and erosion of soil are lessened considerably by shelterbelts.

Figures 5-1 and 5-2 show examples of shelterbelt usage in North Carolina, where loblolly pine does nicely for this purpose because of its configuration and rapid growth.

Like the wind, moisture is affected by the presence of forests. Relative humidity is generally higher in a forest than outside it.

The loss of water by evaporation from the surface soil within forests is much less than that in open-field unvegetative areas. In contrast, transpiration of water from herbaceous materials and the trees (as discussed in Section 4.3) is greater in forests than from open-field vegetation.

5.4   FORESTS HELP OUR WATER SUPPLY

The undisturbed forest floor (*ground litter*) can absorb over 200 percent of its own dry weight in water. Ground litter serves as the horticultural equivalent of mulches. It serves as insulation, preventing the soil surface from heating or cooling excessively, thus effecting temperature control. It conserves moisture by slowing evaporation from the soil surface, and protects the soil from erosion or compaction brought about by pounding rains. Soil water that is not employed for growth of vegetation gradually sinks and becomes part of the underground water supply. Rainwater in excess of that which is absorbed runs off and enters streams and rivers.

Raindrops that strike bare soil dislodge and carry in suspension soil particles, some of which may then clog soil openings. Since much of the surface water then cannot be absorbed, it flows over the ground, carrying some of the soil with it, resulting in erosion. Any material that absorbs the energy in falling raindrops therefore decreases erosion, hence preventing the formation of gullies, paths, or channels worn by water. When the European settlers first arrived, they generally found deep, clear streams. Today many of those streams are silted and shallow, and the water is muddy and subject to great variations in depth, depending upon the rainfall. These new conditions greatly affecting stream quality result from conversion of forests into farmland and loss of reduction in runoff rate formerly produced by forests. Figure 5–3 pictures water quality being examined by a forester.

Through rapid runoff of rainwater toward the ocean and great industrial use of underground water, in many places the water table has dropped and is still dropping. Runoff water from bare land is not entirely wasted because in many cases it is trapped by dams and reservoirs and may be employed for hydroelectric power, cooling of steam-driven electric plants, and irrigation.

5.5   FORESTS AND STREAM FLOW

The flow of water in streams is directly affected by the presence of forests. Stream flow fluctuates primarily with the amount and kind of precipitation—rain, snow, sleet, and hail. The water in streams is

Figure 5-3. Forester studying sample of water to determine quality of this mountain stream. (Courtesy USDA Forest Service)

supplied both by surface runoff (water that passes over the soil surface) and by subsurface flow (water that seeps through the soil). The land area contributing to a stream or river is called a *watershed*.

As indicated in Section 5.4, surface runoff occurs when the ability of the soil to absorb water is exceeded. Excess precipitation fills depressions or low places in the forest floor, such as holes or cavities left by stumps and roots of decayed trees, as surface storage. Also there is interception storage by vegetation, such as shrubs and other plants, and the effect of ground litter, which lessens or checks the rapidity of runoff. Ground litter and humus, decomposed plant and animal residues in the soil, can absorb and hold considerable quantities of water. A portion of the falling rain is intercepted by the crowns of trees and evaporates, thus never reaching the soil.

Snow, which occurs in many of the forested regions of the United States, is a very significant source of water. Figure 5-4 shows a forester measuring a snow pack so as to predict what will happen when it melts. Snow is a form of temporary water storage. Forests retard snow melt in the spring, hence releasing water to streams less rapidly than do open fields, and thus make spring and summer stream flow more uniform. However, an abnormally rapid melt can also result in a flood.

Forests contribute to the regularity of spring and summer stream flow by increasing the proportion of the stream's water that came by seeping through the soil rather than by surface runoff. They can moderate ordinary floods and maintain springs.

Figure 5-4. Forest ranger measuring depth and water content of snow pack. (Courtesy USDA Forest Service)

5.6 FORESTS AND FLOODING

Under normal conditions, streams establish channels sufficient to carry the water discharged into them. However, prolonged torrential rains and rapidly melting snow can fill streams beyond their capacity. The resulting overflow causes damage to property and in some instances loss of human life. Flood damage usually is correlated with population density along main rivers. Rapid rise of water in headwater streams (tributaries) results in flooding of the main rivers, the destruction of bridges, buildings, and roads, and the deposition of debris on land and in buildings.

During our country's development, large areas of forest were cleared from the watersheds of rivers such as the Ohio, Mississippi, Missouri, and Columbia river basins, to make way for farming, industry, and urban areas, thus making them more prone to flooding than before, and local and downstream flood control much more difficult. It became necessary to build levees, usually walls of dirt or of sandbag construction, to prevent excess water from spilling over the banks. Good forest management regulates runoff, which moderates extremes in stream flow in headwater regions and, in turn, helps prevent downstream floods.

5.7 SUMMARY

In this chapter the science called ecology was defined and various aspects of ecology were touched upon, such as the ecology of forest wildlife, the impacts of human activity upon the environment, possible interactions between climate and the forests, water supply and forests, and so on.

Rainfall removes dust from the atmosphere, provides the water necessary for tree growth, replenishes the underground water table, dissolves nutrient materials in the soil, sometimes creates erosion, fills the river headwater streams, and may result in disastrous floods. Lack of rainfall, wind and barren soil caused the famous Dust Bowl.

Forests are affected by climate and in turn produce some effects upon climate. Air and ground temperatures within forests differ somewhat from those outside. Forests affect the speed of air movement. Shelterbelts protect agricultural fields from winds and snowdrifts, while windbreaks protect farmsteads by changing wind direction and reducing wind speed. Ground litter retards flow of rainwater and also serves as a thermal insulator, reducing the rapidity of changes in forest temperature. Excessive conversion of forest land into agricultural fields has contributed to soil erosion, silted streams, and contributed to the need for levees.

chapter 6

Recreational Uses of Forests

> *The forest is more than just trees. It is the raw*
> *material for products we need and enjoy. It is the*
> *livelihood for the people who work in it. It is the*
> *animals, fish, birds and plants that live in it. It is*
> *also the people who hunt, hike, boat and fish in*
> *it, the air freshened by it, and watersheds that*
> *depend on it.*[1]

6.1   THE MOVEMENT OF PEOPLE INTO CITIES

During the eighteenth century, many villages and small towns in
England and other areas of Western Europe became almost deserted
as their inhabitants moved into urban areas. This movement was
mainly due to the growth of industries in which young men could
earn higher wages and gain personal independence, which was more
attractive than life on the farm.

As urbanization developed, people began to realize that they
missed the outdoors, and this led them to seek new activities that
brought them into closer contact with nature. Love of nature is not
a recent phenomenon. People have always liked outdoor activities, and
for almost everyone the dark, mysterious forest has exerted a strong
fascination. However, they also do not want to give up the amenities
of city life.

Urbanization has developed quite strongly in the United States.
It has also become customary to spend as much time as possible in

---

[1] *Forests of the Future*, a pamphlet (New York: Westvāco Corp., 1977),
p. 7.

recreational activities away from home, especially since the automobile has made outings more easily available to a large part of the population. The more crowded our cities and the greater the pollution from factories, the more people like communicating with nature. Outdoor recreational sports and related activities and tourism have flourished during the past 50 years.

Today, millions of people purchase sporting equipment, fishing and hunting gear, and recreational vehicles. The industries that supply skiing outfits, motorboats, and camping, hunting, and fishing equipment employ thousands of workers and produce millions of dollars worth of goods. As a whole, the tourist and recreational industry represents one of the larger branches of the national economy. This industry and the people who participate in outdoor recreation benefit from good forest management.

6.2 POPULATION GROWTH AND RECREATIONAL NEEDS

The forests, rangelands, and inland waters of the United States amount to nearly 1.6 billion acres, and a large portion of this land is used in some manner for outdoor recreation, either primarily or secondary to or associated with another use. The type of use and its intensity varies greatly, from the Arctic tundra region of Alaska with its occasional hunter, to areas of high-intensity use, such as in the state and national parks noted for scenic beauty or developed sites such as ski resorts.

Since our government began to set aside land for public recreation, such as Yosemite National Park (1864) and Yellowstone (1872), the nation's first national parks, the demand for more public recreation areas has grown steadily. Today the U.S. population exceeds 200 million people compared to 4 million in 1800, and, the majority of it is located in or around urban areas. The work week has shrunk from six to four days in some instances. Many workers get vacations that last two weeks to a month or more each year. Several national holidays have been shifted to Mondays so that workers can have three-day weekends. Salaries have increased so that wage earners have excess money left after acquiring their necessities and can spend it on recreational activities. The development of modern appliances and shortcut conveniences has made for more leisure time for most people. Television and other media keep people informed as to what recreational activities are available and their locations.

Forests supply scenic drives, picnicking, hiking, mountain climbing, fishing, hunting, group camping, backpacking, cross-country ski-

Figure 6-1. Nature trail on the banks of South Carolina's Edisto River. (Courtesy of Westvāco)

ing, snowmobiling, motorcycling, canoeing, rafting, and swimming. Several of these activities may be available in the same forest area.

Figure 6-1 shows the use of a nature trail on the banks of South Carolina's Edisto River that winds through a forest that has grown on the site of an old phosphate mill and flooded rice fields from an antebellum plantation. Cypress, pine, and hardwoods are identified along the trail.

U.S. Forest Service forecasts indicate that the demand for recreation will double by the year 2020. The increases will be primarily for the developed types of activities, as opposed to the wilderness type. Figure 6-2 indicates large differences in the sizes of the projected increases. Sailing is expected to quadruple by 2020, while activities like photography, other boating, water skiing, and bicycling will more than double. Activities such as horseback riding, hiking, motorcycling, and picnicking are expected to have the smallest increases.

6.3 PUBLIC RECREATIONAL FACILITIES

Many local governments have provided land for recreation. Parks administered by local government (counties, cities, townships) cover about 1.5 million acres. Parks managed by counties are larger than

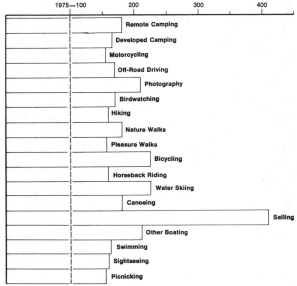

Figure 6–2. Projected indexes of demand for outdoor recreation at year 2020, by major activities. (From *Wilderness Withdrawals and Timber Supply*, National Forest Products Assoc., Washington, D.C., 1978, p. 27)

city parks and usually are in rural areas, which results in more natural settings. However, many well-designed and landscaped zoos and city parks are quite pleasing.

State parks cover 3.5 million acres and most are in forested areas. They attract 350 million visitors per year, the largest attendance being on weekends when people can get away for a day or two. Operational and maintenance funds for state parks come mainly from the state governments, while land purchases usually are paid for by the federal government.

The following federal agencies manage and administer outdoor recreational areas: U.S. Forest Service, Bureau of Outdoor Recreation, Fish and Wildlife Service, Bureau of Land Management, Bureau of Reclamation, Corps of Engineers, and the National Park Service.

Established in 1916, the National Park Service is responsible for more than 30 million acres of the nation's forests and rangelands. It administers 286 locations that have national significance in outdoor recreation, scenery, archaeology, history, biology, and geology. It administers four categories of land: natural areas kept in their natural state, such as national parks and monuments; recreational areas that cater to outdoor activity, such as lake shores, parkways, and seashores; cultural areas, such as Wolf Trap Farm Park near Washington, D.C.; and historic locations, such as major battlefields, historic sites, military parks, and memorials. However, its primary function is in the category of recreation.

Many states offer different ways to view their scenic wonders. Wisconsin has visitors ride in an old steam locomotive train on the site of the Conner Forest Industries in the northeastern part of the state so they can view the old logging areas, museums, and country stores.[2] People also are shown films on the logging industry so that they can be informed of the various steps in the logging process.

Several national conservation groups such as the National Audubon Society, the Sierra Club, and others are active in influencing people to be knowledgeable of their public recreational resources and in the conservation of the natural environment. They want people to enjoy themselves and participate in outdoor activities without damaging the surroundings.

6.4 PRIVATE RECREATIONAL ENTERPRISES

More than 1 million private businesses are associated with outdoor recreation, covering several hundred million acres of land that have more than 800 million visitors a year. Also, thousands of commercial enterprises provide or cater to outdoor sports activities and amusement parks, covering 18 million acres, with several hundred million visitors a year.

Dude ranches, fishing and hunting camps, beaches, resorts, marinas, winter sports areas, and vacation farms comprise thousands of recreational areas with 600 million visitors annually. Frequently, they are in the proximity of national parks and forests. Some commercial outdoor recreation companies cooperate with the forest management agency in protecting wildlife, land, and watersheds, because they realize that these must be taken care of in order for the outdoor recreational locations to be of continuing interest.

6.5 FOREST WILDLIFE AND RECREATION

Animals and birds that roam free in a forest and fish are known as wildlife. Most regions of the United States support a wide variety of wildlife. In the early history of America, wildlife was of major importance as a ready source of food. The forests and surrounding areas supported an abundance of rabbits, squirrels, bears, deer, birds, and fish. Today, hunting and fishing continue, not to provide food for survival but mainly to provide sport and recreation. Most hunters

[2] This idea came from *Introduction to Forestry*, 4th ed., by Sharpe, Grant W., Hendee, Clare W. and Allen, Shirley W., p. 85.

appear to enjoy the hunted wildlife as much for their craftiness, grace, and strength as for the challenge they provide.

Recreational use of wildlife nowadays falls into two categories: consumptive and nonconsumptive. Consumptive uses are those in which hunters kill and use their kill or parts thereof for food, clothing, and/or as trophies. Birds, fish, and other animals hunted for such purposes are referred to as game, wildgame, or game animals. Trends in the populations of game wildlife are quantified in terms of annual harvests (numbers killed).

Nonconsumptive uses are those in which people derive pleasure from observing or studying wildlife and their characteristics through sight, sound, and photography. Figures 6-3 through 6-5 are examples of photographed wildlife. Many species of wildlife, including those of interest to hunters and fishers, thus give esthetic enjoyment to people. They are watched and photographed, listened to, and their sounds are recorded. Many people are content with making general observations and identifying the species that frequent the vicinity of their homes simply by unaided sightings and listening. Others own camping gear, updated field guides, expensive binoculars and photographic equipment, and travel great distances, sometimes braving the wilds to observe new or rare species. The number of wildlife photo-

Figure 6-3. (*Left*) Flying squirrel, showing flaps on body that enable it to glide from tree to tree. (Courtesy North Carolina Wildlife Resources Commission)

Figure 6-4. (*Right*) A black bear cub. (Courtesy North Carolina Wildlife Resources Commission)

Figure 6–5. Wild turkeys cautiously feeding on a wildlife food plot. (Courtesy USDA Forest Service)

graphers has grown to several million, and there are approximately 10 million bird watchers in this country.

An increase in the nonconsumptive appreciation of wildlife is expressed by the following reports: Bird book sales nearly tripled in the first four years of the 1970s; the National Audubon Society dues doubled in the same period. Subscriptions to *National Wildlife* rose sixfold between 1963 and 1975. A periodical of the National Wildlife Federation, *Ranger Rick*, is at present subscribed to by over 500,000 children. It seems probable that many of them will reach adulthood with awareness and appreciation of wildlife.

Nonconsumptive interests in wildlife other than photography and bird watching include listening to the calls of moose, coyotes, and wolves and observing beavers. None of these groups is a separate entity. The avid listener for the moose's mating call would most likely notice a deer browsing in the vicinity. It is likely that the major source of enjoyment is augmented by the tranquil settings of the observing or listening sites.

Our forests have an abundance of beautifully colored birds. These include the vermilion flycatcher, redheaded woodpecker, robin, bluebird, cardinal, and western tanager. These are nongame birds and are not hunted for sport. It is unlawful to kill them.

Of the approximately 20 million hunters in the United States, 8 million seek big game, while the remainder hunt small game. Big game in the East consists of deer, bear, moose, and, in the Smoky Mountains, wild boar. In the West the big game list is much lengthier, including, in addition to the preceding, elk, antelope, mountain goats and sheep, and cougar. Small game are similar in both regions: Rabbit, squirrel, and fox lead the list. A variety of species often regarded as small game but collectively called varmints are, in part, coyotes, prairie dogs, rats, and porcupines. Small game animals classified as fur bearers are harvested primarily by trapping.

Some of the game birds hunted for sport are turkey, quail, grouse, and pheasant. These are dependent upon the forest fringe for food and cover. Ducks and geese are migratory waterfowl. They nest and rear young in the far north during the summer and fly south each winter. Hunting usually takes place during this season of migration, and excellent hunting occurs in the rivers, swamps, and lakes of our forests.

The numbers of both small and big game hunters are increasing. Changes in the distribution of the U.S. population slightly toward more rural areas suggest that there may be continued increase in hunting. With the population moving typically toward the sunbelt, southern states are expected to gain at the expense of the northern and plains states. However, some general public sentiment questioning the moral aspects of hunting has arisen on state and national levels. In the early 1970s reports indicated that two fifths of the residents of New Jersey were against deer hunting. Rather extensive efforts have been made recently to halt all waterfowl hunting. Other influences that could significantly affect hunting are increased urbanization, lack of accessibility to private lands, decline in hunter-success ratios, and restrictions imposed on travel by energy shortages.

There are twice as many fishers as hunters at present in the United States. Thirty-three million persons in the United States were classified in 1970 as "substantial" anglers. This was 21 percent of the population 12 years or older. It is anticipated that the number of freshwater anglers will double or triple during the next 45 years, judging from the experiences of the most recent decades.

Wildlife in danger of extinction are referred to as endangered species, and those likely to become extinct are protected by law, and are thus protected species. Forty species of birds and mammals have become extinct since 1820. At present there are 143 endangered or threatened species of wildlife in the United States. Examples of protected species are the eagle, osprey, red-cockaded woodpecker, and the alligator. Though extinction of species has occurred throughout history for various reasons, there is general agreement among ecologists that human activities related to land development have played a major role in the more recent and accelerated extinctions.

Many species of wildlife perform a vital function in helping stabilize natural systems. They destroy insects and other enemies of the forest and the field. Birds alone are instrumental in eliminating insects that would cause hundreds of millions of dollars worth of damage annually.

Figure 6-6. The forest provides outdoor recreation opportunities for thousands of American fishers daily. (Courtesy of Westvāco)

6.6 SUMMARY

People who live in urban or suburban districts miss the outdoors, and because of the mobility supplied by the automobile are able to satisfy their recreational desires in forested areas on a one-day, weekend, or annual-vacation basis. They engage in observation of scenery, hiking, picnicking, mountain climbing, swimming, canoeing, photography, hunting, fishing, skiing, and the like. The National Park Service administers recreation areas, historic locations, and cultural areas. Many states also invite tourists and provide recreational facilities in their forest and park land. As the U.S. population continues to grow, so also will recreational needs increase.

Wildlife plays a part in recreation. Animals and birds are observed, photographed, and in some cases hunted. Fishing in forest streams is an important part of recreational activity. Some species of wildlife are endangered from one cause or another, usually related to human activities, while those likely to become extinct are in the protected category. In general, the presence of wildlife is beneficial because it preserves an ecological balance in the forest. In some cases hunting is permitted or even encouraged to correct or prevent wildlife overpopulation.

chapter 7

Forests and Our Economy

7.1 TREE GROWING AS A BUSINESS ENTERPRISE

Trees can be planted, grown, and harvested like other agricultural products such as corn, wheat, and cotton, the differences being that crop growth is slower and that most tree crops are not cultivated, though some are. Originally, natural forest stands were so abundant in this country that little or no serious thought was given toward deliberately planting trees to produce a salable crop until about a half-century ago. A first step in production management was taken when lumbermen and perceptive foresters began selecting the trees to be cut and leaving certain ones uncut for seeding purposes. Later came the idea of clear-cutting followed by the planting of seedlings or seeds of species that have commercial value. Forestry has become big business, and timber production plays a major role in the economic structure of the United States. An increase or decrease in timber production has a direct influence upon our economy, and forest management for optimum production now can be quite technical in nature.

Timber production can be increased by management intensification. Opportunities by which gain in production may be achieved lie in a variety of treatments, all of which require the investment of money in labor or materials.

Accelerated Regeneration. When a forest is harvested, its regeneration by nature alone may take decades. Quick and intensive preparation of the site, similar to preparation of a new field by a farmer, followed by planting of nursery-produced tree seedlings, can quickly improve timber production. This practice is increasing rapidly on industrial forests and to a lesser degree on private lands. Each year nearly 2 million acres of forest plantation are established in the United States. Most of this planting occurs in the southern forest (55 percent), followed by the Pacific coast region (22 percent), the northern forest region (13 percent), and the central and Rocky Mountain regions (5 percent). Plantation regeneration will contribute much to our forest productivity.

Water Control. Vast areas of forest land, mainly in the Lakes States and in the Southern Coastal Plain, are so saturated with water through most of the year that tree growth is much reduced. Construction of drainage ditches in such areas can result in significant increases in forest productivity. Although many hundreds of thousands of such acres have been drained over the years, much is yet to be learned of the long-range ecological effects of this practice.

Stand Conversion. Much of the land in all forest regions has, in the past, been misused through growth of less-than-maximum desirability. The brush fields of the Pacific coast, the stagnated stands of lodgepole and ponderosa pine in the Rocky Mountains, and the overcut and steeply graded upland hardwood stands of New England and the South are a few examples where conversion of the growth to a new species or at least a new and better stand of the same species would greatly increase the productivity of the land. However, there are millions of acres of forest land where stand conversion may be neither possible nor desirable.

Stand Improvement. The removal of undesirable stems to release growing space to more vigorous and valuable stems is another route to increased productivity. Prime examples where this is economically feasible are on small, individually owned forest woodlots in the East.

Thinning. The cutting of trees to provide additional growing space so that fewer, but better-formed trees may grow more rapidly. Many species of pines tend to reproduce so abundantly that individual tree growth is stagnated, and the number of years required to produce trees of usable size becomes very great. Thinning can reduce this time.

Fertilization. Operational forest fertilization was first carried out in this country in Douglas fir stands of the Northwest. Nitrogen fertilizer in the form of urea applied periodically has resulted in substantial increases in growth. Much of the soil of the coastal plain pinelands of the Southeast is so deficient in phosphorus that its application at the time of planting results in great increases in growth. Application of potassium to the sandy soils of the Lakes States also boosts tree growth. While fertilization has become routine on many industrial forests, its potential has not yet been fully realized.

Intensified Protection. Three pests, the southern pine bark beetles, the western pine bark beetles, and the western dwarf mistletoe, cause losses equal to 13 percent of the current annual harvest. Creating means to reduce these and similar losses could considerably magnify the production of our forests.

Protection from forest fires has represented a tremendous effort and, for many people in this country, forestry and fire control are synonymous. The acres lost to forest fires have been sharply reduced in the past 50 years. Today the annual wildfire burn of about 5 million acres appears to be holding steady. Only increased understanding of and control over the causes of this steady loss from our forests can reduce it. If it can be done, this lost growth and forest land would be made available to our economy.

The loss of trees to diseases at advanced ages is a natural and ongoing process. Proper management techniques can reduce such losses. We lack, however, the means to protect our forests from the occasional epidemic diseases, such as the chestnut blight, oak wilt, or Dutch elm disease.

Genetic Improvement. Figures 7–1 and 7–2 show the controlled pollination of loblolly pine taking place in a seed orchard at the U.S. Forest Service Lake City Research Center in Florida. Each tree in the orchard was established by grafting onto established loblolly pine root stock a branch tip collected from a mature wild tree that showed superior growth rate, form, or disease resistance. As the grafted trees grow and flower, the female flowers are covered with plastic bags to protect them from wild or unknown pollen, and then are pollinated with pollen collected from other superior trees. Seeds collected from such orchards are then used to establish pine plantations

Figure 7-1. Pollination of female flowers of loblolly pine with male pollen of known parentage. (Courtesy USDA Forest Service)

Figure 7-2. Hypodermic needle employed to inject pollen into plastic bag surrounding female flower. (Courtesy USDA Forest Service)

composed of better-formed, faster-growing, and more disease-resist-
ant trees than can be found in nature.

Forest tree improvement began in 1925 at Placerville, California,
where many conifer crosses were made. Today, in addition to the
work of the U.S. Forest Service, many states and most large forest-
based industries have active tree improvement programs. The more
productive plantations that result from such programs will do much
to meet our country's future needs for wood and fiber.

7.2 FORESTS AND THE GROSS NATIONAL PRODUCT

Each year, officials in Washington calculate an amount of money
called gross national product (GNP). It is their estimate of the total
value of the products that have been produced and the money paid
for services rendered during that year in the United States. This figure is an important measure of the state of the national economy. If
the GNP is divided by the national population, giving dollars per person, this amounts to a direct measure of our national prosperity; the
larger this value, the better off we are in economic terms.

Estimates made from study of all timber-based activities indicate that they supply approximately 6 percent of the GNP and slightly
less than 5 percent of the employment in the United States. Timber-based activities include forest management, timber harvesting, the
initial milling process to produce lumber and other wood products
such as plywood and paper, production of furniture; the building of
houses and other structures, and the transportation involved in moving the material from the harvest area to processing sites and finally
to the consumer. Estimates also indicate that for every dollar's worth
of timber harvested, the resulting product value is approximately $25.

Forestry-related business, which started out with just an interest
in trees, has now grown to a multibillion dollar industry in lumber,
paper, plywood, and all other by-products of wood. These products
are so vast in number that it requires a good amount of time to cata-
log everything that can be gleaned from our wooded land.

7.3 ADMINISTRATION OF AMERICA'S WOODED LAND

Our wooded land is owned partly by commercial interests, federal
and state governments, and private individuals. It follows that public
officials have the task and responsibility of deciding how much logging activity and of what kinds may take place on publicly owned

land when timber is sold to commercial interests, and how much forest land should be reserved or set aside for purposes other than logging, such as recreation, wildlife preservation, hunting, grazing, lake sites, and mining of minerals. These decisions are based upon many factors, such as what the various users are willing to pay and how much is readily available. Political pressures are also sometimes among the factors that will influence such decisions.

For some years it has been basic national policy for public officials to try to arrange for as much multiple use of a given forest area as possible, and to seek for relative amounts of these various uses that will result in maximizing the total public benefit. It follows that it may not be in the best public interest for any particular use to be maximized in a particular forest nor devoted exclusively to it, and that some of these uses may interfere with the timber industry's desire for a total harvest.

7.4 FOREST WILDLIFE AND OUR ECONOMY

The presence of forest wildlife helps the national economy in a number of ways through the industries that support the recreational activities of photographers, bird watchers, listeners, hunters, fishers, and so on. Outdoor recreational activities provide employment and income in some rural areas where other opportunities are limited or nonexistent. The ability to travel has stimulated the building of parkways and superhighways. Trapping of animals and selling their pelts is still big business in some states. The principal animals whose pelts are used in the fur industry are mink, muskrat, raccoon, otter, opossum, skunk, weasel, and fox. Millions of dollars are made each year on the sale of animal skins. The number of trappers varies with the demand for furs.

Hunters spend about $2 billion annually in the United States. Big game hunters average 7 days annually in the field and spend $122 per person, amounting to $953 million. Small game hunters average 11 days annually in the field and spend $81 per person, amounting to $946 million.

The license fees collected from hunters and fishers and the excise taxes on firearms, ammunition, and fishing tackle support the major cost of maintaining fish and wildlife populations; about 85 percent of the cost of state fish and game agencies is supplied by these sources. Wildlife research programs, improvement of habitat for wildlife, and the costs of administrative controls have been totally supported by these monies.

Finally, as stated earlier, wildlife of some species, particularly birds, kill insects that would otherwise damage or kill trees or farm crops and in that sense contribute to the national economy.

87
Forests as Sources
of Energy

7.5   FORESTS AS SOURCES OF ENERGY

As stated in Section 4.3, trees, in the process of growing, utilize solar energy to assist in the manufacture of wood fiber, thus storing that energy. Coal and oil also contain solar energy that was captured and stored millions of years ago. Coal, oil, and natural gas are regarded as nonrenewable energy sources because of the amount of time required for their natural replacement. Wood, however, is regarded as a renewable resource. An acre harvested of trees can produce another crop of trees in a relatively brief time.

Trees have been used for energy since people first learned to use fire. As late as the early twentieth century, more wood was cut in this country for fuel than for any other purpose. Even now fuel is the leading use for wood in a number of nonindustrialized countries.

Today, in face of shortages and the soaring cost of fuel oil, many industrialized countries are again looking to wood as a source of energy. There is less energy in a pound of wood than in a pound of coal or oil, and the presence of water reduces the available energy even more.[1] On the other hand, wood is less expensive, and its smoke contains only slight amounts of the oxides of sulfur and nitrogen, which are serious air pollutants associated with fossil fuels. However, unless carefully burned, wood can produce undesirable amounts of particulate matter (small solid drops of organic matter and ash).

Wood can be burned in a number of ways, as solid wood, as chips, or as pellets. Home fireplaces, wood stoves, and some industrial furnaces burn solid wood. Chips are produced in the woods by powerful machines that can reduce in less than a minute a large tree, limbs, bark, and leaves into small slivers of wood about the same size as a paper match book. Chips may then be burned in modified boilers to produce steam. Several industries and institutions about the country have converted to chip burning as a source of energy. In Vermont, chip-fired boilers are driving turbines to produce electrical energy for a local power company.

---

[1] Oven dry wood contains about 8,500 Btu per pound, coal has about 12,000 Btu per pound, and fuel oil averages 19,000 Btu per pound. One Btu, which stands for British thermal unit, is the amount of energy required to raise the temperature of 1 pound of water 1° F.

Wood pellets are formed by putting scraps and waste wood into a hammer mill, which reduces it to a coarse-textured dust. This is then mixed with a bonding agent and compressed into small cylindrical pellets of dry wood fuel. The process may require and use almost 20 percent as much energy as the pellets contain. Nevertheless, the hot clean fire from pellets and their ease of handling recommend them for certain uses.

When charcoal is produced, the volatile portions of wood that are drawn off are flammable gases, largely methane and carbon monoxide. This process, called destructive distillation, is an ancient one but is being restudied. Also still experimental are the production of wood alcohol as a fuel by fermentation of wood and the chemical hydrolysis of wood into hydrogen gas.

It would not be possible to supply all the country's energy needs from wood without quickly destroying its forests. It will be possible to supply part of it and thereby reduce our dependence upon fossil fuels and create a desirable diversity in the total energy picture.

7.6   THE PRACTICE OF FORESTRY AS A CAREER

Of the 25,000 people who made a living through forestry in 1976, about 40 percent worked in private industry, chiefly for lumber, logging, or pulp companies. Another 25 percent were in government employment, most of them working in the U.S. Forest Service of the Department of Agriculture. The remainder were in the employ of state and local governments, consulting firms, colleges and universities, or were self-employed, either as consultants or forest owners.

As of 1980, fifty colleges and universities offered education in forestry leading to the bachelor's degree or an advanced degree. Forty-three were accredited by the Society of American Foresters. Since much of the forester's work today involves the application of scientific knowledge, the minimum educational requirement is a bachelor's degree with a major in forestry. In fact, because of the increasingly complex nature of the forester's work, many employers prefer graduates with advanced degrees. Research work and teaching jobs require advanced degrees.

Generally, new forestry graduates work under the supervision of experienced foresters. During the initial phase of their careers, many do much of their work outdoors. They manage, develop, and protect forest lands and resources. The young forester's general activities include mapping the locations and estimating the quantities of resources

Figure 7-3. Wildlife clearing developed to provide food and cover for forest game. (Courtesy USDA Forest Service)

such as timber, wildlife, water, forage, and recreational areas. They specify locations that need treatment with pesticides for control of insects and disease. They determine areas that need to be reforested, and they also make decisions concerning the thinning of dense stands and pruning of trees.

Foresters may also plan and supervise the harvesting methods employed, which range from selective cutting to clear-cutting. They plan logging operations according to soil conditions, slope, wildlife requirements, and visual effects. Foresters become involved in wildlife protection (see Figure 7-3), watershed management, and coordination of the activities of fire-fighting lookouts, patrollers, and pilots who are engaged in detection and surveillance of forest fires. They develop and supervise hiking trails, camps, parks, and grazing lands.

Foresters also note rare and endangered species of plants and animals and unique or unusual ecological conditions of trees, shrubs, and flowers. They give talks to campers, rescue climbers and skiers, and locate hikers and rafters who are lost or stranded.

The forester may employ computers to assess data and engage in aerial photograph interpretation. There are foresters who have specialized in wood technology, the study of its structure, identification of physical, mechanical, and chemical properties, defects and uses, and processing characteristics of wood. In fact, some foresters are engaged in research that goes deeply into the basic physical and biological sciences. They work with many of the most modern devices in technical laboratories, wood preserving plants, sawmills, pulp and paper mills, plywood and particle board plants, and furniture factories.

Foresters are in demand as speakers for various groups, ranging from primary school classes to service clubs and scientific organizations, and thus supply forestry information to the general public as well as to forest owners. Some foresters are engaged in a specialized area of work, such as forest economics, timber management, outdoor recreation, or forest engineering. Some teach in colleges and universities.

7.7 FOREST AND LOGGING ENGINEERING

A special branch of forestry is forest engineering, sometimes called logging engineering. This work consists of the design and construction of buildings, roads, bridges, and dams. In planning a harvesting or logging system, the forest engineer's expertise is used in the design, selection, and installation of equipment for moving logs and pulpwood out of the harvesting area. Soil types, terrain features, and types of equipment to be used are crucial considerations prior to a logging operation. For example, in critical terrain regions such as mountains and swamps, road construction may be too expensive or unacceptable in relation to preventing soil erosion, protecting streams and rivers, or preserving scenic resources. In such a situation the forest engineer would most likely select a more feasible logging system that employs helicopters, balloons, or skyline cable systems. Forest and logging engineers may be graduates of forestry schools that offer courses in logging engineering or they may be graduates of schools of engineering.

7.8 THE FOREST TECHNICIAN

Forest technicians in most forestry organizations are people with aptitude and experience whose formal education went little beyond the secondary school. Sometimes referred to as forestry aides, often they have graduated from curricula in technical schools or community colleges. The skilled work of the forest technician requires aptitude, experience, and training, but not the professional and academic education of the forester. People who are happier with continuous outdoors work and constant contact with the forest may find the forest technician's work more appealing than that of the forester. In addition, those who prefer one locality to being transferred to other places or positions may find the life of the technician more attractive.

The number of forest technicians employed the year around in 1976 in the United States was estimated at 11,000. Approximately the same number were employed part-time by state and federal governments in the summer months or during the fire seasons of spring or fall. The U.S. Forest Service that year had 3,700 full-time forest technicians in its employ, while state governments had 2,200.

About 80 technical schools, community or junior colleges, and universities offered technical training in forestry in 1976, and the Society of American Foresters recognized 53 of these. The curriculum at most of these schools included general education courses such as English, mathematics, biology, and botany, as well as specialized forest technology courses such as land surveying, tree identification, aerial photograph interpretation, and timber inventorying and harvesting. Forest technicians often are also required to attend a forestry camp operated by the school. A growing number of high schools throughout the country are offering an introductory level of technician training.

7.9 SUMMARY

Our forests and their products play a significant role in development of the gross national product (GNP) through production of materials and employment of people. Forest-related recreational activities also help the GNP both directly and indirectly. In the near future our economy may be significantly further aided through fuel energy derived from solar energy obtained by biomass production.

Forest management today is to a large degree directed toward more intensive multiple-use utilization of both publicly owned and privately owned forest land. Intensification of timber production is based upon eight or more policies and purposeful activities. These require investment of money, which gives modern forestry the character of a business enterprise. Privately operated recreational activities also are businesses.

People who make a living directly through forestry contribute to the GNP. They generally have had training in forestry. A full-fledged forester has a college degree and, in many cases, graduate education as well. The professional forester starts with practical experience in all phases of work in the forest and later engages in management, planning, and research. A forest engineer specializes in the design and construction, at minimum cost, of the facilities needed for logging. Forest technicians generally are people who enjoy outdoor work. Many of them have had two years in a technical school after high school.

chapter 8

Forestry Abroad

8.1 TREE DISTRIBUTION FACTORS

The conditions under which trees grow are established locally and they vary widely all over the world. The Northern Hemisphere contains the bulk of the world's land area that has a temperate climate; therefore, the coniferous forest is largely found there. The richest mixture of broadleaf species is found mostly in the warmer, damp, regions, and therefore the tropical forest areas are made up almost exclusively of broadleaf species. In regions where two climatic zones meet, mixed broadleaf and coniferous forests are found. The conifers, with a few notable exceptions (mainly the pines) are most typical of the cooler, higher altitudes.

Trees, like animals and humans, are always in competition for food and living space. So it can be understood that trees will thrive where the climatic zone, water, and soil are best suited for them. Many factors are involved in the distribution of trees. Seeds can be carried by winds, or downstream on a river, or by birds and animals, and thus find their way to the most unlikely places. The fruits of certain trees are eaten by birds and the seeds are eliminated from their bodies in their feces; as a result, in the United States, the eastern red cedar, whose succulent cones are a favorite food of many birds, is frequently found along fence rows and underneath telephone lines where the birds have perched.

Some trees cannot exist under constant shade; others cannot live without shade. A tree may stop growing when other trees around it cover its crown; but when the adjacent trees are removed the covered trees start to grow again. Trees that need light, especially those that have lightweight seeds, often grow on clear-cut land or on abandoned farms or new river margins. As mentioned in Chapter 4, most trees will die if their oxygen intake is interrupted; some can grow successfully on wet or periodically flooded areas.

8.2 WORLDWIDE FOREST RESOURCES AND PRACTICES

Forest resources and forestry practices vary greatly throughout the world. Some countries have no specific forestry organization and hardly any commercial operations or forest conservation program. Other areas in the world are well aware of the importance of forests and have been practicing forest management for centuries. More than 40 countries are conducting some kind of forestry work. The major part of foreign forestry practice is located in the following countries: Canada, Brazil, Norway, Sweden, South Africa, Russia, China, India, Indonesia, Australia, and New Zealand.

Approximately 28 percent of the world's land area, an estimated 9.2 billion acres, is under forest cover. The timber inventory for the world's forest is estimated at 12.6 trillion cubic feet (0.357 trillion cubic meters). About one third of this forested land area supports softwood forests, while two thirds supports hardwood forests. The major portion of the hardwood forests is in the tropical regions of Africa, Southeast Asia, and Latin America. Most of the softwood forests are concentrated in the Soviet Union (1,366 million acres) and in North America (1,087 million acres), with all the other countries claiming only 525 million acres. Nearly 85 percent of the total volume of timber taken from the world's forests comes from North and South America and the Soviet Union. Approximately 83,860 million cubic feet (2,361 million cubic meters) of timber was cut throughout the world in 1970. Roughly 54 percent of this was for industrial use and the rest was cut for domestic uses and fuel.

Forest products are important to international trade, especially raw cut lumber. Pulpwood for use in producing newsprint and paperboard is also a very important world trade product. Predictions indicate continuing increases in European demands for pulp and paper products produced in the United States. In regard to lumber and poles, however, projections indicate that most of the growth will be supplied by imports from Canada, the USSR, and tropical hardwood regions. The developing countries of Africa and Asia have a large volume of export trade in logs. They have substantial forest resources and are adopting forest practices developed elsewhere.

China has about 200 million acres of forest land, and its government is becoming more aware of the importance of practicing forestry. China's large number of organizations engaged in planting and raising trees indicates the spread of forestry practices there. Replanting and maintaining forest land devastated by many blights and wars are part of the forestry program in China today. A major effort is their attempt to build the world's largest shelterbelt system.

Japan's phenomenal economic growth in the last 20 years has resulted in immense increases in industrial wood consumption, sixfold from 1950 to 1972, reaching 3.6 billion cubic feet (102 million cubic meters) roundwood equivalent (logs). Although Japan's forests have been well managed for centuries, they were heavily depleted by overcutting during World War II. Japan has an approximate forest area of 48 million acres. However, to meet rapidly increasing demands, Japan imports great volumes of both softwood and hardwood. Logs and other wood product imports amounted to 2 billion cubic feet (57 million cubic meters) in 1972.

According to the Japanese Forestry Agency, demand for timber products will continue to increase to about 4.8 billion cubic feet (136 million cubic meters) by 1981. About 63 percent of this projected demand is expected to be met by imports. An increasing share of Japan's total demand is expected to be supplied by Japanese forests in the late 1980s. Japan also imports a large volume of wood from the Australian state of Tasmania, the forest industry of which we shall now discuss as a foreign example.

The forests of Tasmania are more important to its economy than are those of any other Australian state. The per capita value of forests in Tasmania is more than four times higher than elsewhere in Australia. Industries that depend upon Tasmanian forests produce more wealth than those dependent upon any other form of land use. The wood chip industry has become a thriving business in

Tasmania since 1971, when a 15-year commitment was made to export to Japan nearly 3 million green tons annually through 1986. These chips, used for pulp, will have a total value of about $550 million.

The total annual lumber production in Tasmania, about 14 million cubic feet (400,000 cubic meters), nets an annual income of about $40 million. After satisfying the local needs and those of the other states of Australia, surplus lumber is exported. Lumber cut from Tasmanian tree species is used for paneling and flooring. Tasmanian oak is the trade name for lumber cut from three almost identical species of eucalyptus, which comprises almost 90 percent of the lumber production of Tasmania. Figure 8–1 shows a young Tasmanian forester when in the U.S.A. on a visit.

Australia's government and that of New Zealand encourage good forest practices and employ a staff of professionals on a civil service basis. Both countries are noted for very modern and intensive practices.

The USSR has an estimated forest area of 1.5 million acres, of which less than one half is easily accessible. Large areas of land are not used for agriculture, yet do not have any trees on them. Much of the wood cut in Russia is used for firewood. The USSR is a large exporter of coniferous logs and lumber.

Canada, the leading timber exporting nation of the world, sends 75 percent of its export timber to the United States. Canada's geographic and economic ties to the United States make it a primary timber supply region. One fourth of Canada's land area, about 600 million acres, is forest. More than 19 million acres of National Parks

Figure 8–1. B. M. Collins in conversation with young Tasmanian forester, Alan Castley, on the right. (Courtesy Sherwood Githens, Jr.)

and 5 million acres of Indian reservations are controlled by or are under the jurisdiction of the Canadian government. Prince Edward Island is the only province that does not have a Forest Service. Most of the Canadian universities offer forestry courses, forest products industries being of strategic importance to that country.

The tropical countries of the world are rapidly increasing their forestry activities. While the teak plantations of Indonesia have long been a noteworthy example of tropical forestry, there is also an intense concentration on forestry in South America. Brazil is an outstanding example of a country having both traditional and totally new activities. Vast plantings of exotic pine and eucalyptus species and several native tropical hardwoods grow at incredibly rapid rates. These supply fiber to a growing pulp, paper, and lumber industry. In addition, the steel mills of Brazil, which has little domestic coal, are fueled by charcoal made from wood, and most of Brazil's cars and trucks are currently fueled with alcohol, which can, in part, be made from wood. Although extensive clearing of tropical forests is a matter of considerable controversy, the tropical countries are pioneering new techniques in forestry and uses of wood.

8.3 FORESTS AND FORESTRY IN EUROPE

Of all the European countries, Finland and Sweden have the highest percentage of forest land. Sweden has a total productive forest area of 57 million acres, covered chiefly with Norway spruce, white birch, and Scotch pine. Forests thrive in Sweden because its soil and climate are conducive to forest vegetation.

Sweden had a national forestry school organized as early as 1835. Because Sweden's forest industry is so large, the high schools specialize in training students for technical positions in forestry, and several colleges offer courses in forestry. The Institute of Forest Management also trains specialists to manage harvesting operations.

In Finland, forests are the mainstay of the economy. In fact, it is called "the land of forests and water." Over 75 percent of the total area of Finland is forested. Pine and spruce comprise about 80 percent of these forests and birch constitutes most of the rest.

Switzerland can be credited with some of the earliest efforts in forestry in the world. Specific forest regulation ordinances date back to 1304 in the Canton of Berne. Zurich had the first working plan for its Sihlwald (city forest) in 1680. As early as 1491, the year before Columbus discovered America, the boundary lines were marked off, making it one of the oldest examples of forestry. Tree felling is rigidly controlled in Switzerland because of the steep mountains and possible soil erosion if trees are removed. Most Swiss forests are classified as protection forests, from which wood cutting can be done only under strict supervision by foresters. Similar rigid conditions are exercised throughout much of Germany.

8.4 RECREATIONAL USE OF EUROPEAN FORESTS

Students hike their way through Europe and elsewhere during the summer, backpacks on their shoulders, with very little money in their pockets, walking through the national forests, learning first-hand the history they have studied in books. Special maps are given out so that hikers may explore the forests of the Alps in Germany and Austria, taking days to complete their journeys, stopping at various rest areas along the way. This is indeed the ultimate nature hike in the world, because one covers two countries or more if feet and legs can take it.

Cross-country skiing in the Nordic countries is one of their greatest attractions, people coming from all over the world to compete in races and in sporting events. Without the forests, these activities could not exist. Skiing, tobogganing, and other winter sports are on the rise around the world. With the advent of the three-hour jet trip to Europe, some people think nothing of gathering their ski equipment and taking a weekend trip to one of the mountain forests of the globe.

8.5 INTERNATIONAL FORESTRY ORGANIZATIONS

In 1892 the International Union of Forestry Research Organizations was established in Vienna, Austria. Its prime objectives were to stimulate interest in research in forestry and to start international studies of important tree species and programs for testing timber internationally. This world organization of forestry committees moved its headquarters to neutral countries during the Nazi take-over of Europe in World War II. Currently, Union congresses are held at 5-year intervals, and over 22 committees in special areas of forestry coordinate progress in research in their fields.

After many changes in organization, the Food and Agriculture Organization (FAO) was adopted and became a member body of the

United Nations. It has a Forestry Division. In 1973 the headquarters of the Forestry Division of FAO, located in Rome, employed approximately 61 forestry specialists who were experienced professionals, many of whom were citizens of the United States. Funds for the FAO program come from a biennial assessment on member countries according to an agreed-upon formula. Initially, the United States was responsible for one third of the biennial budget. In 1972, Congress changed this by limiting the U.S. contribution to 25 percent effective January 1974.

The responsibilities of the Forestry Division of FAO are promotion and coordination of research among the member nations; dissemination of statistics on forest area, timber value, and growth; protection of international trade in forest products; advisory functions to member nations, especially where one nation has developed techniques of value to others; and cooperation with other public international organizations.

The U.S. Agency for International Development (USAID) has helped many nations financially to establish forestry curricula in their colleges and universities. An example is the Philippine College of Forestry, operated with assistance from Syracuse University's New York College of Environmental Science and Forestry. The recipient country is required to finance at least one half of the project's cost. Foreign companies have assisted by giving sites for research in the more valuable and readily accessible portions of their timber holdings.

The International Union of Societies of Foresters was organized in 1969 in Washington, D.C. Its main reason for being is "to promote international cooperation for the advancement of the practice and profession of forestry and of professional foresters throughout the world." As of 1973, more than 19 nations' professional forestry societies were participating.

8.6 SUMMARY

Many factors govern whether a particular region will or will not be forested. Most of the world's land having a temperate climate is in the Northern Hemisphere, and there the forests are largely of coniferous species. The warmer, damper regions tend to be tropical in nature and hardwoods predominate. About 28 percent of the world's land area is forested, and of these forests, about one third are mainly softwood and two thirds mainly hardwood. Forest products today play a large part in international trade. The United States buys a large part of the output of Canada's forests. Japan has become a heavy buyer because of immense increases in industrial consumption of wood. However, Japan is endeavoring to grow more wood. Tasmania is an example of a Southern Hemisphere district where lumbering and chip production are major industries under government encouragement and management.

Forestry practice of the Western world got its start in Western Europe several centuries ago. Sweden and Finland are leaders in production.

Germany and Switzerland, each with a very small amount of forest land, practice a sophisticated and intensive form of multiple-use forestry in order to gain maximum wood, recreation, game, and watershed benefits.

International organizations for forestry are helping the developing countries improve and enlarge their forests by supplying funds to help operate forestry schools and experienced teaching personnel. Such schools train and prepare individuals in the practices of modern forestry.

chapter 9

The Practice of Silviculture

9.1 SILVICS AND SILVICULTURE

A forest can grow without any help from people, but greater amounts of wood can be grown in less time with applications of the current scientific advances and technology. Our accumulated knowledge permits intelligent use of the forest, the ability to shape nature and to avoid waste resulting from poor planning or inadvisable cutting. Foresters today employ their knowledge of silvics and their understanding of the forest as a plant community to more successfully manage wooded areas. This knowledge was gained by patient observation of forest growth and through research.

Silvics, defined in Section 4.5, consists of those parts of the biological sciences that relate to forest ecosystems. In essence, silvics consists of the life history and general characteristics of forest trees and stands, with particular attention paid to environmental Influences.[1]

Silviculture was also described in Section 4.5. It has been defined as "the art of establishing, developing, and reproducing

[1] These ideas came from *Forestry and Its Career Opportunities*, 3rd ed. by Shirley, Hardy L., pp 98-99.

forests." A more modern general definition favored by many foresters is "the systematic management of forests, including all the manipulative operations involved in development and maintenance for producing high yields of forest crops through applications of knowledge of silvics."[2] For example, controlling or stopping an insect epidemic would be as much a silviculture practice as is the thinning of trees. From this standpoint, silviculture includes subject matter discussed not only in this chapter but also in other parts of this book.

The silvicultural practices to be employed by a forest owner require consideration of such characteristics as type of forest, its age, species makeup, climate, and soils, together with the owner's projected goals. The following examples of silvical characteristics affect the management of a particular kind of forest or species:

1. Tolerance to shade
2. Wind firmness
3. Tendency to grow in a mixed or a pure stand
4. Growth patterns (e.g., even-aged or all-aged stands)
5. Degree of difficulty in obtaining reproduction

Forest owners who desire financial gains from certain kinds of products, such as Christmas trees, recreation, or sawlogs, must decide upon which silvicultural treatments shall be employed. Many practices associated with the growth of commercial timber crops are on a rather solid foundation. This is because costs and responses to treatments can be reasonably estimated prior to many operations, and rational projections can be made about the financial returns.

Silvicultural treatments related to wildlife-carrying capacity, increased water yields, recreational benefits, and environmental amenities have been less well studied than those related to timber growing. But such treatments have been objectives of foresters working in both the public and private sectors. Inability to measure recreational and amenity values and unstable responses to surveys have impeded evaluation processes.

With respect to shade from sunlight, tree species can be classified into three types, referred to as intolerant, moderately tolerant, and tolerant. The tolerant species are able to reproduce and grow in a fashion normal for that species with only small openings in the canopy. The intolerant species reproduce satisfactorily only if they have full sunlight. They cannot tolerate shade.

[2] Ibid.

It has been emphasized that forests are "renewable" resources; if the trees are cut down and their wood is used, new trees will grow in their places, which is not the case when coal is mined or oil is pumped out of the ground. The trees reproduce themselves, particularly with some help from people, utilizing energy from the sun, which we can regard as an inexhaustible energy source. The sun is expected to last for billions of years.

Forest trees are produced from earlier growth in four main ways:

1. By seedlings planted by hand (Figures 9–1 and 9–2) or by machine (Figure 9–3)
2. By seeds planted by people
3. By seeds fallen from trees
4. By vegetative means, from stump sprouts or shoots or root suckers

Figure 9-1. (*Left*) Planting tree seedlings by hand in Arkansas. (Courtesy of the Weyerhaeuser Co.)

Figure 9-2. (*Right*) Hand planting a Douglas fir seedling in Washington. (Courtesy of the Weyerhaeuser Co.)

Figure 9-3. Planting tree seedlings by machine in North Carolina. (Courtesy of the Weyerhaeuser Co.)

Seedlings and seeds usually are planted by hand. Machines are employed when the area is so large that it would be impossible to do the planting in a short amount of time by hand. Machines can plant seedlings at a rate of 1,000 per hour if the land is free of standing trees, gullies, stumps, and rocks. The high rate of planting accomplished by these machines lowers the cost compared to that of hand planting but may increase the costs of land clearing prior to planting.

Young plants must be protected from damage by fire, diseases, and especially insects, which are capable of defoliating whole forests in some cases. A planted area is checked 1 year after, and if the percentage of survivors is too low, the area often is replanted.

An important new aspect of silviculture is fertilization. Substantial gains in heights and diameters have been observed on some sites with some species of trees from application of nitrogen or phosphorus. In critical areas subject to severe sheet erosion, such as gullies and mine spoils or where the topsoil has been removed, a cover crop may be planted and fertilized prior to planting trees. A supplement to this may be to mulch severely damaged soils with pine or wheat straw after tree planting.

Trees may be planted to establish a new forest stand, called a *plantation*, where no forest land had previously existed or to replace a forest that has recently been harvested. Very occasionally, planting may be done in an existing stand to ultimately change its composition.

Though most forest trees are very effective at reproducing themselves naturally, planting, often called artificial regeneration, offers several advantages. First, it is much quicker; effective natural regeneration may take several years. Second, the forester may ensure that only the desired species is established. Third, and perhaps most importantly, the forester can plant just the proper number of trees so that space is not wasted by having too few and growth is not retarded by having too many.

Tree size and age of the trees to be planted depend upon the species and the means of production. Tree seedlings are produced in tree nurseries, some large enough to produce millions of seedlings a year (see Figure 9-4). Seeds are planted to germinate in uniform rows, and the seedlings are carefully tended with irrigation, fertilizer, and pesticides. The seedlings may be removed from the beds, a process called *lifting*, at the end of the first growing season, or if their growth is slow, at the end of the second, but rarely more. Sometimes they may be moved to transplant beds to grow even older and stronger. A new and growing practice is to germinate a single seed in a small plastic or fiber container. Many thousands of such containers are held in greenhouses as shown in Figure 9-5, until the seedlings are ready to be moved to the forest site for planting.

Figure 9-4. Ponderosa pine seedlings at the Klamath Fall, Oregon, nursery. (Courtesy Weyerhaeuser Co.)

Figure 9-5. Containerized seedlings in a greenhouse. Each small white cylinder contains a single seedling. (Courtesy Weyerhaeuser Co.)

For each region of the United States a technical guide is available giving appropriate details on soil and site preparation. It will also name species well adapted to the region, suggest desirable spacing, and so on. Such guides are available at county offices of the Soil Conservation Service and the office of the local county agricultural extension service.

Most stands of trees have originated from seedlings, planted seeds, or seeds dropped beneath a parent tree or carried to the site by winds, streams, birds, or animals. Vegetative reproduction, on the other hand, called *coppice growth*, results from dormant buds located on stumps left after tree cutting, or from buds developed on roots close to the ground surface, as seen in Figure 9-6. Both bud types produce successful stands, but stump sprouts may be subject to early rot if they are too high on the stump or if they are on very large stumps. Often these new trees are poorly spaced because of the spacing of the old stumps.

Vegetative reproduction progresses quickly because of food supply left in the stump and root systems. However, coppice growth is subject to being deformed and frequently the resulting trees do not represent top quality. An exception however is that many of the redwoods are of coppice origin and are of acceptable quality. Coppice growth is also quite vulnerable to catastrophic events such as high winds, freezing rains, and floods because sprouts shear off easily at the point of attachment to the old tree growth.

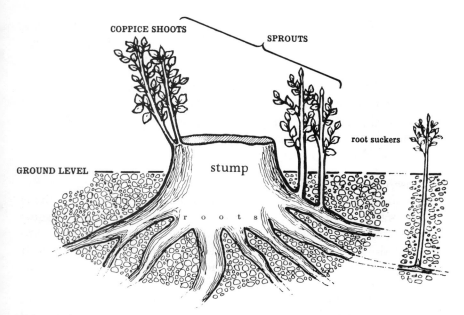

Figure 9-6. Forms of vegetative reproduction of trees. (From F. C. Ford-Robinson, ed., *Terminology of Forest Science, Technology, Practice and Products,* Society of American Foresters, Washington, D.C., 1971, p. 310.)

A coppice or copse is a thicket or grove of small trees originating from sprouts, roots, or stumps. When stand reproduction is based entirely upon sprouts, this aspect of silviculture is called the coppice system of reproduction.

9.3 CREATING A NEW STAND

To establish a forest of a desirable kind where it does not at present exist may require three steps: (1) clear-cutting of an existing stand, (2) conditioning of the soil to provide the proper root environment and space in the sun for the desired species, and (3) reproduction by direct seeding or planting. Clear-cutting allows for establishment of new trees without their being influenced by previously existing trees, and the resulting stand will be even-aged. Having a clear-cut site may be unintentional because complete destruction of all or a large portion of a stand may occur naturally from insects, disease, fire, flood, wind, and so on.

In the event that brush, weeds, or grass are present on the land to be planted, site preparation of some kind may be desirable to reduce the future competition for sunlight and moisture. Preparing the site for new growth is important. Three steps in site preparation are the following:

1. Control of nontree plant species that may compete with the future crop or modify its environment.
2. Removal, reduction, or piling of debris (slash) left after a previous stand of trees has been felled.
3. Preparation of the soil.

All these operations may be accomplished through the use of herbicides and heavy machines that both break down dead or living organic material and turn over the soil. The debris left after a logging operation may be physically detrimental to tree reproduction or to the operations required to make and tend a new stand of trees. It may also be a fire hazard, because the small pieces of wood, limbs, and leaves dry quickly and may burn readily.

Fires have been used for site preparation, since natural fires have been observed to create good conditions for regeneration and growth of new forests. Forest managers must be careful in using fire. It is not safe in some locations because of fuel conditions or because the terrain is too steep or irregular for proper control of a fire. Mechanical site preparation may be practiced in these cases. Logging operations can also aid in site preparation, because through the use of skidding equipment the log movement can eliminate vegetation and break down the debris left from the felling of the trees.

Figure 9–7 shows a debris-crushing machine at work on a site in Arkansas in preparation for planting a new stand. Figure 9–8 shows a bedding plow at work in a clear-cut area. A bedding plow is employed in intensive site preparation on low-lying lands that tend to be very wet. The plow raises a bed above the general soil level for better drainage. The bed is then planted with seedlings of a suitable species.

9.4 HARVEST CUTTING AND STAND RENEWAL

Sometimes trees are cut simply for stand improvement. More often cutting takes place as a harvesting operation, with close attention paid at the same time to stand renewal and improvement. The cutting methods employed in forest management are regarded as a part of silviculture. If proper cutting methodology is employed in the management of a forest stand, reproduction of desirable tree species

Figure 9-7. Site preparation by use of crushing machine, in Arkansas. (Courtesy the Weyerhaeuser Co.)

Figure 9-8. Bedding plow used in site preparation before planting in a clearcut area in the South Atlantic coastal plain. (Courtesy the Weyerhaeuser Co.)

Figure 9-9. Area devastated by loggers in clear-cutting a Douglas fir forest in 1940. (Courtesy of the Weyerhaeuser Co.)

may be obtained, as well as control of tree density, quality, size, growth rate, and maximization of yield.

The number of years between the establishment of a crop or stand of trees and its final cutting at a specified stage of maturity is known as the *rotation* period of tree growth. This number of years will vary widely for various species and locations, and will depend upon many factors.

Figures 9-9 and 9-10 are photographs taken at the same place in Wolf Point near Longview, Washington, in the years 1940 and 1960. The first shows the land immediately after a clear-cutting of Douglas fir. The second shows a new forest of Douglas fir 20 years later. At the projected rate, foresters expect to harvest again in the 1990s. Thus, this area is on a 50-year rotation. A clear-cut in the South, regenerated with fast-growing pine species, could be harvested twice in the same time period, thus permitting a 25-year rotation.

Clear-cutting. As a method of harvesting, clear-cutting has some advantages: Today, wood chips and pulpwood are often so valuable that everything cut can be sold, removal from site is simplified, and an excellent stage is set for stand renewal. Adequate reproduction

Figure 9-10. Same area as in Figure 9-9 twenty years later, regenerated in Douglas fir. (Courtesy the Weyerhaeuser Co.)

may be obtained by beginning the harvest at about the time seed fall begins in a good seed year. However, the most certain way to obtain reproduction is to plant a desired species after cutting. Site preparation often is necessary for the establishment of desirable reproduction.

Seed-tree Cutting. Scattered groups or individual trees are left standing in the cut-over area to provide seed. Even-aged stands result from this style of harvesting. The seed trees should be carefully selected to be the best of the stand and be well distributed over the cut area. Site preparation is often necessary before and after cutting to ensure adequate reproduction.

Shelterwood Cutting. The mature stand is cut in a series of two or three partial cuttings, which provide spaces for reproduction. Fairly even-aged stands result from this procedure. In southern pine, prescribed burning as site preparation often is necessary prior to cutting to ensure establishment of reproduction.

Selective Cutting. Selective cutting is the annual or periodic removal of trees, particularly the mature individuals or small groups from an uneven-aged stand, in order to get a better yield.[3] The oldest and largest trees are removed periodically, with reproduction becoming established in the openings made by these cuttings. A modification of this method is group selection, where groups of trees are cut, providing large openings and more light. The forest as a whole is divided into nearly equal parts, and an individual part is selectively cut each year in a cutting cycle. Site preparation is not often practical when the selection method is employed.

Coppice Cutting, with Standards. Some high-quality trees (standards) whose origins were from seeds are left standing while the remainder of the stand is cut, and reproduction is obtained through sprouts from the stumps. The standards protect the site and produce high-value products. The standards are preserved for at least two coppice rotations. This system, of course, only works with species and ages capable of producing vigorous coppice sprouts.

9.5   INTERMEDIATE (IMPROVEMENT) CUTTING

Seedlings and saplings have problems in growing because of trees that grow above them. This may require a *cleaning* operation, removal of undesired species or poorly formed individuals of a desired species. Such cuttings are made in young stands in the sapling stage or younger. *Stand improvement* is the phrase employed if the stand of trees is older.

Liberation cutting is the removal of undesirable older, larger trees that have been left from the preceding stand and may be overtopping the desirable trees. Liberation cutting normally results in financial cost, but if the larger trees are salable, these cuts may yield a return.

Pruning is another intermediate operation, not often practiced in forests. It is the altering of the form of specific trees, rather than their complete removal. These cuttings are made in an immature stand to increase the quality of production. For example, improvement of stem wood is attained by cutting all the lower branches of trees so that more clear or knot-free lumber is produced. Christmas-tree shaping is achieved by cutting off branch ends.

[3] F. C. Ford-Robertson, ed. *Terminology of Forest Science, Technology, Practice and Products* (Washington, D.C.: Society of American Foresters, 1971), p. 233.

Salvage cutting is performed when trees have been killed or damaged by insects, fires, disease, or other natural disaster. Such trees are removed to recover some of the loss and to possibly forestall outbreak of an epidemic.

Thinning or forest density control is the most used of intermediate silviculture operations. Thinning is the adjustment of numbers of trees in a particular stand in order to concentrate the growth capability of the land on the remaining trees so that they may grow strong and tall and will be more valuable. The removed trees usually are not in a dominant position in the stand. Thus, thinning may result in the harvest of some trees that would be lost because of inadequate soil, water, and sun. *Low* thinning is removal of the smaller individual trees, which leaves the larger ones more room. *Crown* thinning is freeing the crowns of the best and biggest trees. *Precommercial* thinning is the cutting of trees too small to be marketable. Figure 9–11 shows workers in a thinning crew receiving instruction from a forest manager.

After thinning operations are completed, the remaining trees are in optimum condition to make use of additional nutrients and crown space. Aerial fertilization is employed by forestry firms to supply the nutrients needed for faster growth. The kind of nutrient to use, whether it be nitrogen, phosphorus, or some other chemical element, is indicated by soil tests on the areas concerned.

Figure 9–11. Workers in a tree-thinning crew in western Washington receiving instructions from a forest manager. (Courtesy the Weyerhaeuser Co.)

9.6 SUMMARY

Forest owners and managers, combining knowledge of silvics with good judgment, practice silviculture to produce desirable and valuable tree stands. Tree regeneration can be based upon either clear-cutting and total replanting to ensure reproduction or upon periodic cutting of part of a stand and continuous reproduction. Silviculture operations include timber cutting; site preparation, which may include removal of debris, ground breaking, and fertilization; seeding or planting; protection from insects, animals, and disease; thinning; pruning; sanitation cutting; liberation cutting; protection from fires; the use of herbicides to eliminate competing vegetation; and so on. In brief, silviculture includes all the steps taken so trees can grow and mature in minimum time.

chapter 10

Forest Measurements

10.1   FOREST MEASUREMENTS DEFINED

Forest measurement or mensuration is concerned with making evaluations and estimates that are required in the management of forest land and in connection with all the products and services derived from such land. Forest measurements are mathematical in nature, being concerned with numerical values obtained from use of instruments or by estimation.

   Forest measurement has to do with the ages, diameters, heights, volumes, rates of growth, and land areas of standing timber. It has to do with the volumes and growth of logs, pulpwood, fuel wood, chips, and single pieces, such as posts, poles, piling, mine props, and railroad crossties. The most recent aspect is the measurement for possible use of all the plant material on the site (biomass). It also encompasses surveying or measurement of land on which forests grow. Forest mensuration as a science perceives the forest as a dynamic community that can lose by damage, is reduced by harvest, and gains by growth. Thus it is an element in maximizing multiple use of forest land.

10.2 NECESSITY FOR FOREST MEASUREMENTS

Many people are concerned with the adequacy of the use of our forest land and want to make sure it produces a maximum of wood and related services useful in our livelihood. With continuing increase in the value of forest products, more attention is being paid to accurate forest measurement.

Measurements play a significant role in the management of a forested area, with the intent to achieve such objectives as the production of more wood, forage, game animals, water, or recreational benefits. Periodic inventories of forested land are required for determining amounts and quality of wood available for yearly use, for tax records, and for justifying management expenditures. The sawtimber, pulp, and plywood industries have become more adept at using various qualities of wood for different products; hence log weighing has become a common practice. In brief, measurement is a strategic part of forest management.

10.3 MEASUREMENT OF TREE DIAMETER

The diameter of a tree is most commonly determined at breast height, which is an established reference point (standard taken at $4\frac{1}{2}$ feet (137 centimeters) above average ground level. The *diameter breast height,* abbreviated dbh, is taken outside the bark to the nearest 0.1 ($\frac{1}{10}$) inch (.25 centimeter) when making volume-growth determination, and to the nearest 2 inches (5 centimeters) when estimating total volume of a stand, which is a close-enough measurement in that case. In instances of abnormal growth shapes, leaning trees, and trees growing on slopes, adjustments are made in measuring diameters to avoid any unusual influence on the measurement, as indicated in Figure 10-1.

In measuring tree diameters the basic instruments are referred to as *dendrometers.* The three most common ones are (1) the diameter tape, (2) the tree caliper, and (3) the Biltmore stick. The instrument selected for use usually depends upon the degree of closeness of measurement desired, the convenience of the use of the instrument, and the place on the tree to be measured.

Trees are not perfect cylinders. The diameter of most trees is greater in one direction than in another, and the trees taper and become narrower in the vertical direction. These irregularities in shape necessitate measuring both the short and long diameters and averaging the two measurements to obtain the average diameter. An error in diameter measurement may have a great effect upon the computa-

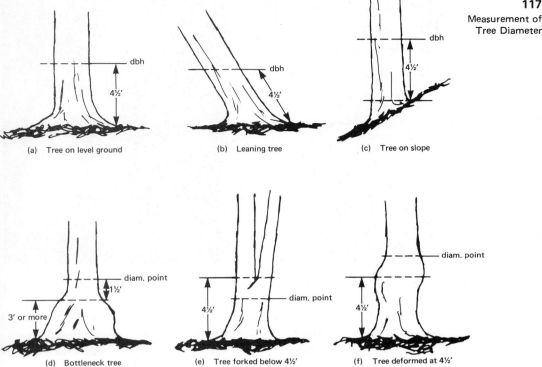

Figure 10-1. Points of dbh measurement for sloping-ground or irregular stems.

tion of volume; a 1-inch (2.5 cm) loss in diameter measurement has the same effect as an 8-foot (2.4 meters) error in height measurement.

The diameter tape is a device for converting the circumference of a tree to its diameter, and its readings are direct and precise. The tape may have a bark hook at its zero end. As shown in Figure 10-2, correct use is to hold the case in the right hand with the winding handle up. When the tape is pulled tightly around the tree, the diameter scale is right side up and the diameter value lies directly below the zero of the scale. A common length is 20 feet (6 meters), scaled on one side in feet, tenths, and hundredths of feet to indicate circumference, and on the other side to give diameter equivalents in inches and tenths of inches up to 76.5 diameter inches (194 cm).

The tree caliper is made either of wood or metal and provides a quick and simple method of measuring dbh on trees that are nearly cylindrical. It is a rather simple device consisting of a bar and two legs, one fixed and the other free to slide along a graduated scale on the bar. When the legs are located tightly against opposite sides of a tree, the instrument gives measures of dbh to the nearest tenths of

Figure 10–2. Correct use of the diameter tape. (Courtesy USDA Forest Service)

an inch. Calipers are used conveniently for trees up to about 20 inches (50 centimeters) dbh. For bigger trees, the diameter tape is preferred because large calipers are cumbersome and awkward to handle.

The Biltmore stick was designed by C.A. Schenck for use by his students in the first forestry school in the United States, the Biltmore Forest School near Asheville, North Carolina. Schenck called it the "Biltmore stick" after the name of his school. (The site of this old forestry school and its general proximity are often referred to as "the cradle of forestry in the United States").

The standard Biltmore stick is made of wood, 25 or 30 inches (63.5 or 76.2 cm) long. It is so scaled that when held horizontally against a tree trunk at the customary height ($4\frac{1}{2}$ feet or 137 cm) with the cruiser's (timber volume inventory specialist) eyes 25 inches (63.5 cm) from the tree, the diameter may be read to a closeness of 1 inch for smaller trees and 2 inches for larger ones. The observer must hold his or her head still until the left end of the stick is exactly in line with one side of the tree, as illustrated in Figure 10–3. The graduation which is then in line with the other side of the tree corresponds to the diameter. The diameter scale is marked in inches in $\frac{1}{2}$-inch (1.27 cm) steps.

The Biltmore stick is not an accurate instrument because the 25-inch (63.5 cm) distance from the eye is difficult to control, but it is convenient to use. It is accurate enough for dbh measurements in

Figure 10-3. Use of the Biltmore stick to measure dbh (Courtesy USDA Forest Service)

estimating 1-inch (2.54 cm) and 2-inch (5 cm) diameter classes if it is employed carefully. Many experienced timber cruisers can estimate a tree's diameter within an inch or so, but they usually check their accuracy with one of the instruments discussed in this section.

10.4   MEASUREMENT OF TREE HEIGHT

Many types of instruments have been developed to measure tree height indirectly from the ground; the four most commonly used are the (1) Merritt scale on a Biltmore stick, (2) Abney level, (3) Haga altimeter, and (4) Suunto clinometer. We will discuss only the first two.

Height-measuring instruments are referred to collectively as *hypsometers.* Those used in measuring tree heights employ visual sighting and elementary trigonometry involving angles and sides of triangles. However, the word hypsometer is also applied to a device used in geology for measuring elevation above sea level by observing the temperature at which a particular liquid boils. (It is believed that Elisha Mitchell, 1793-1857, of the University of North Carolina was employing precise surveying equipment rather than a boiling-point hypsometer when he declared what we now know as Mount Mitchell to be the highest point east of the Rockies.)

When the Biltmore stick is employed as a hypsometer, it is held the same distance from the eye as when used to measure diameters.

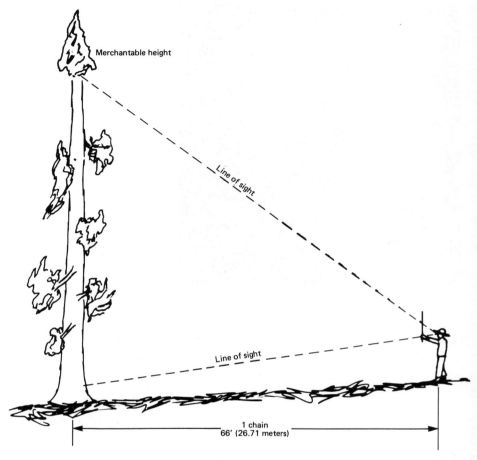

Merchantable height

Line of sight

Line of sight

1 chain
66' (26.71 meters)

Figure 10-4. Employment of Merritt scale on a Biltmore stick to estimate height of a tree.

As shown in Figure 10-4, the zero or bottom end is held so that it intercepts the line of sight between the eye and the stump height of the tree. Without moving his head or the stick, the cruiser makes a second sighting to the merchantable top of the tree. The point at which the line of sight intercepts the scale indicates the tree's height, in feet, meters, or 16-foot logs. Two sets of scales enable readings to be made at distances of 1 or $1\frac{1}{2}$ chains (1 chain is 66 feet or 20.1 meters) from the tree. Where the tree height is too great, the distance from the tree is doubled and the reading is doubled. Heights may be measured on a slope, provided that the appropriate horizontal distance from the tree is used.

The Abney level, named after a British physicist and astronomer, is a clinometer (measures inclination) employed both in surveying and forestry. It consists of a short telescope, a bubble tube (spirit level), and a scaled vertical arc. The forestry models have a topographic scale and a percent scale. The topographic scale is employed with instrument located a horizontal distance of 1 chain (20 meters) from the tree. The percent scale is employed with the instrument 100 feet (30.5 meters) of horizontal distance from the object whose height is to be measured. If the tree top is hidden in a dense canopy or the tree is very tall, an observation may be made at a distance greater than 66 feet (20 meters), and the calculated height value is enlarged proportionately to obtain the actual height.

The principle of operation is explained by use of Figure 10-5. Suppose that the observer levels the instrument by means of the bubble tube when at the distance B from the tree. Then, using the telescope, the observer aims the crosshair at T, the top of the tree. The number then read from the scale is associated with the inclination angle, a. It is *both* (1) the trigonometric *tangent* of a, and (2) after multiplication by 100, the *percentage* of the distance B equal to the vertical distance H being measured. For example, if the arc scale reads the value 0.25, then tan a = 0.25, and H = 25 percent of B, or 25 percent of 100 feet, which is 25 feet. Expressed in an equation,

$$H = (\text{tangent } \angle a) \times B = (0.25) \times (100 \text{ feet}) = 25 \text{ feet}$$

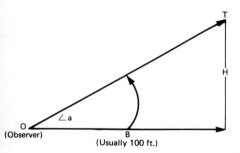

Figure 10-5. Basic geometry and trigonometry associated with the Abney level.

When an Abney level is used, the observer's elevation may not be the same as that of the base of the tree. Four possibilities are sketched in Figure 10-6. In case (a), where observer and tree base are virtually at the same level, one reading suffices. In cases (b), (c), and (d), two vertical-distance determinations are made, which may be called X and Y. Letting H stand for the height of the tree,

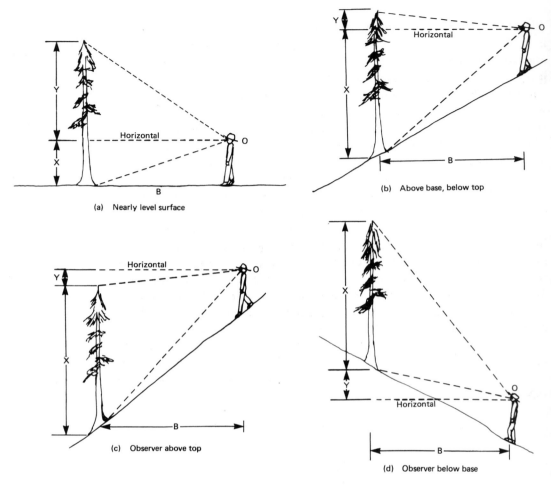

Figure 10-6. Four possible elevations of observer when Abney level is employed.

If elevation O is *between* top and base, $\qquad H = X + Y$

If elevation O is *above* top or *below* base, $\quad H = X - Y$

10.5 MEASUREMENT OF TREE AGE AND GROWTH RATE

Common methods for determining the age of a tree are to study (1) annual growth rings, (2) whorls of the branches of some species, and (3) general appearance, particularly that of the bark. In Section 4.2 how a tree forms annual growth rings by adding a new layer of wood just under the bark has been discussed. A felled tree's age can be determined by counting either the dark or the light rings. Extra rings *may*

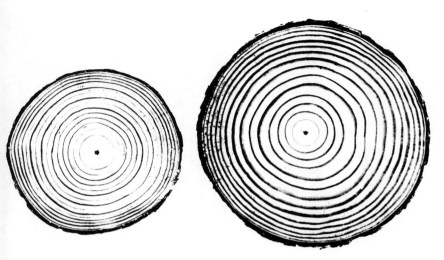

Figure 10-7. Cross sections of two loblolly pines photographed simultaneously, of nearly the same age. The smaller one, 18 years old, grew in a natural stand; the larger, 16 years old, grew in a plantation and had the benefits of good management. (Courtesy American Forest Institute)

be formed during a single year as a result of abnormal changes in weather conditions that temporarily alter growth. Such rings are referred to as false rings and usually are less well defined than the annual rings. Sometimes the false rings do not completely encircle the tree. By closely studying the rings an experienced observer can learn much about the tree's environmental history. Figure 10-7 illustrates a marked difference in growth rate revealed by annual rings.

Growth in diameter varies directly with the spread and the surface of both the crown and roots of a tree. Hence, the major factors that influence diameter growth are age (or size), adequacy of moisture, availability of soil nutrients, proper stand density (whether the tree's neighbors crowded it or shut out its light), and damage from fire, insects, or diseases.

The forester can determine the age of a tree without felling it by employing an increment borer. This hollow instrument is gradually twisted into the trunk, as seen in Figure 10-8. As the leading edge is forced toward the center, it cuts a core of wood, which is removed by use of an extractor, as seen in Figure 10-9. The tree rings are counted on the core, as shown in Figure 10-10.

Increment borers are also employed to determine tree diameter growth for specified periods, such as 5- or 10-year periods, for volume growth determinations. The radial growth (core taken on one side of

Figure 10-8. (*Left*) Insertion of core borer. (Photo by Thomas Wilkinson)

Figure 10-9. (*Right*) Extraction of the core. (Photo by Thomas Wilkinson)

Figure 10-10. Counting rings by use of a core borer. (Courtesy USDA Forest Service)

tree) is doubled to convert it to diameter growth. White chalk spread on cores taken from hardwoods and then rubbed off makes the rings stand out so they are more visible.

Whorls of branches may be used to determine the age of small trees in those species of conifers, such as white and Scotch pines, that produce only one whorl per year. In large trees the positions of upper whorls are difficult to determine, and often bark overgrowth obscures the position of earlier whorls, making whorl count difficult.

Sometimes rough approximations of age can be made by appearance alone, though not very reliably. Experienced observers can determine whether a tree is mature or overmature by studying the bark and tree crown of some species.

10.6 MEASUREMENT OF TIMBER STAND VOLUME

In earlier years when timber was plentiful, neither buyer nor seller paid much attention to the accuracy of timber measurement, but such casualness is now a thing of the past. Today it is important to be able to closely estimate the amount of useful wood material that can be obtained from a particular timber stand or shipment of felled timber. This means that a timber cruiser must make a detailed record of what he or she observes and measures, and must be able to determine quite closely the nature and amount of lumber, pulpwood, or other forest products that can be processed from the timber listed.

Timber cruising usually is carried out on a sampling basis because it would be too costly to measure every tree. Several methods of arriving at a choice of trees that will yield a representative sample have been worked out and are applied where appropriate. The sampling crews employ tally sheets on which to record information about the trees they choose to observe and measure. A tally sheet basically is a two-dimensional chart consisting of vertical columns and horizontal rows that form "pigeonholes" in which tally marks can be entered. For example, the chart may list tree heights (or log counts per tree) in uniform steps in one direction and dbh values in uniform steps in the other direction.

Once the owner, buyer, or seller has in hand the data obtained by cruising or by measurement of the logs in a shipment, he or she then needs to have a good estimate of the marketable product derivable from those logs. The estimate is made by use of a *log rule,* a formula or table that gives, from the diameter and length of a log, an estimate of the amount of lumber that can be cut from it. On the other hand, the cruiser may determine its cubical measure (volume) from its dimensions. The owner, buyer, or seller is thus supplied with cubic volume data.

Not all of a log can be used for lumber because the log is not square and it also is tapered. The first cuts by the saw remove what is referred to as *slab.* As the saw passes through the log it produces sawdust, and the thickness of this cut (producing the sawdust) is called the *saw kerf.* As the outside edge of each board or plank is trimmed, *edging* is removed.

The *board foot* is the traditional basic unit of sawn timber. It is by definition a piece of green, rough-sawn wood 1 foot long by 1 foot wide by 1 inch in thickness. However, after finishing and planing, the 1-foot width and 1-inch thickness are reduced. Thus, a 2 x 4-inch stud is about $1\frac{1}{2}$ by $3\frac{1}{2}$ inches in cross section, but is still referred to (and charged for!) in terms of its rough-sawn dimensions.

The *cubic foot* is becoming more used, and it is probable that ultimately the metric *cubic meter* will be employed in the United States. Conversion from cubic feet to cubic meters will be quite simple and easier than from board feet to cubic meters. (A volume of 35.1 cubic feet equals 1 cubic meter.)

Log rules (tables) give the estimated or calculated amount of lumber in board feet that can be sawed from logs of a given length and top diameter inside the bark. Close approximations of board-foot yield or of cubic volume provide a basis for sales and wage settlements, which in many instances need to be known in advance. By having a means of gauging the amount of lumber that may be sawed out of logs of known sizes, there is no need to segregate the logs of each owner at the sawmill in order to make payments on the basis of a daily mill tally (count of boards cut from logs). That is still sometimes done, but it is awkward and expensive.

Pulpwood usually is cut from sound, reasonably straight trees. In the South the sticks are sawed in 5-foot 3-inch (1.60 meters) lengths, with a minimum of 4 inches (10.2 cm) diameter outside the bark at the small end. Elsewhere in the United States other standards of length and diameter are employed. Today, pulpwood is bought and sold by weight, by cubic feet, by the cord, and by *cunit* (the equivalent of 100 cubic feet of wood).

A shipment of wood intended to be used as fuel, and in some cases pulpwood, is measured by the *cord.* A standard cord is a stacked pile 4 feet by 8 feet by 4 feet high, that is, 128 cubic feet. The actual solid wood volume in such a pile is around 75 to 100 cubic feet. Since 1 cubic foot of water weighs 62.4 pounds (28.3 kilos) and common air-dried wood is a little less than one half as dense as water, it follows that a cord of firewood weighs about 3,000 pounds or 1½ tons (1361 kilos).

Gross weight is now almost universally employed as a means of measuring pulpwood and logs that are to be sawn into dimension lumber. Weight scaling ensures that the seller is paid for the total wood mass delivered and that its measurement is done quickly. The buyer is ensured of getting fresh wood, because it weighs more than dry wood. Conversion tables are employed to convert gross weight into more conventional units. It is likely that weighing and occasional check scaling will become the normal procedure at most wood-buying centers.

10.7 SUMMARY

Forest measurements are evaluations of standing timber as potential produce materials and estimates of growth in relation to land areas. They play significant roles in forest management that lead to maximum utilization of the forest land. Measurements derived through the use of instruments yield numerical values. When measurements include the passage of time, the values obtained are time rates, such as, for example, of biomass production in tons per acre per year.

Tree diameters are routinely measured by dendrometers: diameter tape, tree caliper, and Biltmore stick. Tree heights are measured by optical devices and trigonometry. Tree volume is estimated from values of diameter and height using printed tables. The age of felled trees is determined by counting rings in a stem cross section, while age and diameter growth rate of standing timber are found by increment borer. Tree age can also be judged fairly accurately by experienced foresters by simply examining the trees.

chapter 11

Harvesting of Tree Crops

11.1 PLANNING FOR THE HARVEST

Logging is the term commonly employed in referring to the harvesting of timber. This activity may include felling, limbing, bucking (sectioning of tree stems into manageable lengths), and transportation to sawmills or other processing plants.

When a timber harvest is going to take place, a *logging plan* usually is prepared. Prior to harvest from national forest land, these plans may include a description of the location of the place to be logged, design of a road system for removal, and methods of harvesting considered best economically and ecologically. The logging plan is also involved with factors that include soil conditions, slopes, overall wildlife requirements, and visual effects. Buffer strips in which no cutting is to take place often are left along streams and generally along roads. These provide escape cover, den trees, and food for wildlife. Undisturbed strips along flowing streams prevent siltation by serving as silt screens or filters and supply shade that keeps the water cool for fish. Buffer strips also maintain visual quality along streams and highways.

The logging plan should identify the intended market, the approximate number of hours required for felling, bucking, loading, and transportation, and the personnel assignments for the various jobs involved. The plan is also concerned with the equipment needed, maintenance of the equipment, what alternate plans to use if the equipment fails, and a very important factor, the safety precautions to be taken for the personnel on the job. The logging plan should also describe the follow-up work (contract agreements) needed on the harvest site to reduce erosion after harvesting; for example, skid roads with more than 15 percent grade should be cross-ditched, and all roads, road banks, landings, and loading areas should be seeded to grow cover grass and game food plants.

The logging foreman should have a thorough understanding of the costs of these operations. His responsibility includes supervision and direction of all phases of the work so that it will move smoothly and the costs be minimized. Coordination of these numerous and varied operations requires specialized skill.

11.2 MANUAL FELLING OF TREES

The feller's most basic skill is the ability to cut trees safely and efficiently. The aim is to bring down a tree so that it will not fall against another, will not break when it falls on uneven ground, and after falling can be trimmed of branches (limbed), cut or bucked into logs, and skidded or dragged to a landing with the least obstruction. For many years the tool employed in the United States was the crosscut saw, shown in Figure 11-1. Felling is now done commonly by means of a chain saw (Figure 11-2).

The side of a tree that has the heavier part of the crown, and the direction in which it leans, usually determine which way it will fall. The making of an undercut (removal of a wedge-shaped section of the trunk) in exactly the right place and to the right depth, resulting in a hinge action when followed by a backcut will guide the tree almost exactly to where it should fall. Figure 11-3 is a diagram showing these cuts.

The exact dropping of a tree is very important for several reasons. If the tree falls the wrong way, it may injure other trees, which should be left to grow, or it may break or bend other trees that were not to be harvested, or it may be caught or snagged in the crown or branches of a standing tree. Such a situation can be dangerous for the loggers. At the least, such mishaps cause loggers to lose time and thereby increase costs.

Figure 11-1. A 17½-foot redwood felled by crosscut saw in 1933. (Courtesy Georgia Pacific)

Figure 11-2. A loblolly pine felled by chain saw. (Courtesy USDA Forest Service)

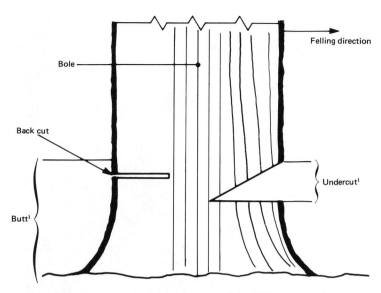

Figure 11-3. Undercut and backcut employed in felling a tree by crosscut saw or chain saw.

Stumps should be cut close to the ground to avoid wasting good wood and so that they do not get in the way of the rest of the operation. To ensure that the loggers do take these precautions, penalties are imposed as incentives so that the loggers are extra careful in the felling operations.

After a tree is felled it may be limbed and bucked, that is, cut into logs or pulpwood *bolts* of desired lengths.

11.3 MECHANICAL FELLING OF TREES

In some cases felling is accomplished mechanically by means of hydraulic-powered machinery capable of working through a thick forest, crawling over rough rock outcroppings, climbing 35-degree slopes, and shearing trees at ground level with great speed. A *shear* (Figure 11-4) is capable of handling trees of 20 inches (50 centimeters) stump diameter or bigger. The direction of fall is controlled by the wedge action of the scissorlike blade. A *feller-buncher* (Figure 11-5) grabs the tree with two hydraulically powered solid arms, shears it at ground level, then lifts and bunches (piles) the felled tree. A *Bush combine* is a machine that shears and bucks trees into 6-foot lengths.

Figure 11-4. Tractor-mounted, hydraulically operated shear felling a tree. (Courtesy the Caterpillar Co.)

Figure 11-5. A feller-buncher felling a loblolly pine. (Courtesy the Caterpillar Co.)

11.4 SKIDDING FROM STUMP TO LANDING

One end of the felled tree is lifted by some form of tractor with a lifting attachment and is skidded across the ground from the stump to a *landing,* where it may be sorted into species or quality classes and loaded onto trucks or chipped and blown into covered vans. In the United States the most common log skidders are four-wheel-drive machines that articulate (are hinged in the center), with wide wheelbase and short turning radius, and a winch that feeds a heavy cable through an elevated fairlead to elevate the front end of the logs. Figure 11-6 shows such a skidder in action. Figure 11-7 shows a similar machine, known as a grapple skidder, equipped with a rotating knuckle boom and hydraulic tongs, which enable the operator to pick up and bunch logs for skidding. Rubber-tired machines are more mobile and can travel faster than crawlers (tractors with tracks), moving at speeds up to 20 miles per hour along graded skidways. When tree-length logs are skidded to the landing, they may be sorted and bucked either into sawlogs or pulpwood lengths or are chipped. In many cases, tree-length logs are loaded onto trucks and taken to mills to be sorted and processed. Figure 11-8 shows a tree-length mill yard near Creedmoor, North Carolina; Figure 11-9 shows a wheel-type tractor at the same yard with a grappler attachment preparing to unload a whole truckload of tree-length loblolly pine.

Mobile in-woods chippers sometimes work directly at the harvest site, as illustrated in Figure 11-10. These reduce whole trees

Figure 11-6. Rubber-tired articulated skidder in operation in Oregon. (Courtesy the Caterpillar Co.)

Figure 11–7. Skidder equipped with rotating knuckle boom and hydraulic tongs with which to bunch logs. (Courtesy Weyerhaeuser Co.)

Figure 11–8. Tree-length mill yard near Creedmoor, North Carolina. (Courtesy Champion International Corp.)

Figure 11–9. Tractor with grapple attachment preparing to unload tree-length loblolly pine trees. (Courtesy Champion International Corp.)

Figure 11-10. Truck-mounted chipper reducing a log into chips and blowing them into covered truck, which will haul them to a paper mill (Courtesy Westvāco)

into tiny pieces and utilize almost all the tree, other than roots and stumps, eliminating much of the waste associated historically with timber harvesting.

Log removal by helicopter and balloon is now occasionally employed where soil and/or topographical problems combined with high timber values warrant the cost of using such a system. It is the exception, however, in the United States.

In some timber operations the practice of *cable skidding,* or yarding to a steel spar, is employed. Cable skidding has been a practice in steep terrain for many years, particularly in Europe and countries such as Australia and New Zealand. Of the two forms of cable skidding, high-lead cable skidding and skyline cable skidding, only the second will be discussed here.

Skyline cable skidding is diagrammed in Figure 11-11. Two vertical spars, both held erect by means of steel guy lines, are employed. One within the cutting area is movable and the other is at the landing. A skyline extends from the top of the spar at the tree-cutting site to a pulley close to the top of the landing spar and then to the yarder engine, which keeps the skyline taut. A steel cable extends from a drum on the yarder engine to a skyline carriage, which hauls the load toward the landing, while a second cable attached to another drum goes by means of other pulleys to the skyline carriage and serves to pull the carriage back to the cutting site after the logs have been dropped at the landing. At the skyline carriage the main line passes around a pulley wheel, then around another wheel at the bottom of the carriage, so that when the main line is pulled taut, the first thing it does is to elevate the load up to the skyline carriage, and

SKYLINE CABLE LOGGING (generalized)

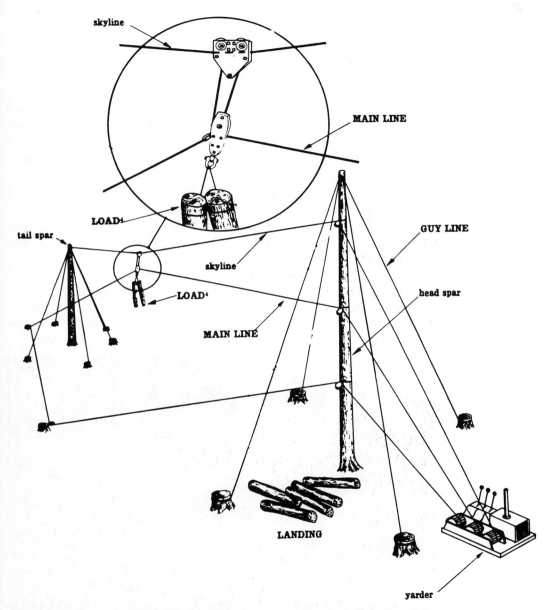

Figure 11-11. Diagram that describes skyline cable logging. (From F. C. Ford-Robinson, ed., *Terminology of Forest Science, Technology, Practice and Products,* Society of American Foresters, Washington, D.C., 1971, p. 315)

then pulls the assembly toward the landing at the head spar. Short chains or cables called chokers are looped around the logs to attach them to the cable system.

11.5 LOADING AND TRANSPORTATION OF LOGS

In the past, loading of logs onto vehicles for transportation usually was done by workers using a *peavey,* a stout wooden level 2½ to 8 feet (.75-1.5 meters) long, fitted into a tapered steel socket terminating in a spike and hinged hook at its far end. This operation involved rolling the logs up inclined skids from the ground onto a truck or flatbed railroad car by means of a cable that passed under the center of the log and doubled back over the vehicle to a source of power, usually animals, a winch, or a tractor. The peavey was used at the ends of the log to keep it from losing or gaining distance on the opposite end, causing the log to stay straight while the cable rolled the log up the inclined skid.

Today most loading onto vehicles is done mechanically. In recent years, huge forklift-mounted loaders have been increasingly employed, as have been hydraulically powered grapplers. Versatile tracked and wheeled tractors with a variety of attachments (Figures 11-12 and 11-13) have simplified and greatly improved the tech-

Figure 11-12. Heel-boom loader and portable steel spar power unit employed in steep terrain in western United States. (Courtesy the Caterpillar Company)

Figure 11-13. Catlift truck unloading pulpwood from truck and loading it onto a railroad car. (Courtesy the Caterpillar Company)

niques of loading. The range of attachments now available includes log, lumber, and pulpwood forks and wood chip buckets. Some of the track and wheel loaders with forklift or grappling attachments can load or unload virtually the entire contents of a log or lumber transportation vehicle in one grasp or scoop.

Sawmills are seldom close to where timber is felled, and many forms of log transportation are employed in the United States. In years past, water transportation was the dominant mode, requiring only a small investment to improve streams for the floating of logs. Today, due to environmental constraints very few logs float to riverside mills, and the romantic spring drive when northeastern rivers were dammed with logs is largely a thing of the past. However, the great inland waterways maintained by the Corps of Engineers have led to a great increase in log and pulpwood movement by barge.

When moved by barge, logs may travel anywhere from 100 to 1,000 miles (160 to 1,600 kilometers).

A large amount of logs and pulpwood is transported by rail, often 200 to 300 miles (320 to 480 kilometers). However, today trucking is the most common way to haul logs from forest to mill. Figures 11-14 and 11-15 illustrate truck transportation of logs.

Figure 11-14. Tree-length logs on their way to the mill by truck. (Courtesy Weyerhaeuser Co.)

Figure 11-15. Truckload of pulpwood brought to be loaded onto a railway flat car. (Courtesy Champion International Corp.)

Contracting for all the phases of logging has been the trend in recent years. The contracts are based either on thousands of board feet, on cords, or on cubic feet. Logs may be scaled (measured) at a location that depends upon the terms of the contract, the payment of the timber fellers, and the type of log transportation employed. It may be done either before they are skidded to a landing, on the truck that transports the logs, in the mill yard, or in a sorting pond. The logs can also be scaled as they enter the mill on a conveyer belt or jack ladder.

Each log is numbered or marked by the scaler. This number is placed in a scale book, with its volume shown opposite it. Two measurements of diameter of the small end of the log are made and averaged if the cross section is irregular in shape. The length of the log may be checked by tape measurement. The log's volume is then determined from a table in a *log rule,* a book of tables, from the scaled diameter and length.

A scaler must know how to recognize defects in a log, to determine the species from the bark or wood, and be familiar with all the customs and laws that are concerned with log specifications.

The logging camps of yesteryear are realistically depicted in the movies, with crude cabins or tents for the muscular men who worked there. Early logging was marked by the necessity of being away from one's family. The long periods of time required for felling operations made for limited social conditions for months on end. These deprivations caused mercurial frustrations that resulted in heated confrontations among the loggers. Modern transportation and housing conveniences have given today's logger a mobility like that of an 8-to-5 worker, and have all but eliminated the social problems faced by the early loggers. America's loggers are no longer isolated in the far woods away from all civilization.

Portable camps are still used in some regions, particularly in the Northwest. Buildings are designed and sized so that they can be shipped on railway flat cars or trucks with trailers, and can accommodate four to eight workers. The dining rooms or huts are large and built in sections.

11.8 SUMMARY

A correctly managed forest has its crop harvested when it is economically and biologically ripe, through a series of planned operations. In the case of tree removal from publicly owned land in particular, the plan must include a number of postharvest operations that will leave the land in first-class condition. The use of modern methods of felling, limbing, bucking, skidding, loading, and transportation to the mill result in maximum efficiency and yield. Today, trees are felled by chain saw or perhaps by a hydraulic shear. Skidding to the landing is done by machinery. The manager of the harvesting process must be knowledgeable and the workers skillful.

Modern timber harvesting, particularly in the West, may be carried out with each step in the process paid for by contract based upon the amounts of wood involved. These amounts are determined by scaling of diameter and length and computation of the yield, with each log numbered and entered in a log book. Scaling the raw product works out to be better for contracting purposes than tallying the final products.

chapter 12

Insects and Diseases

12.1 DAMAGING FORCES

Forests have countless enemies. Some are living creatures; others are natural elements, such as ice and snow that lie heavily on branches, crushing crowns and breaking trunks. Large sections of forest growth can be wiped out by strong winds. Vast areas of forests have been buried by shifting sands. Floods, erosion, cold, frost, and drought can virtually eliminate entire forests. In addition to damage done by climatic forces, harm is caused by insects, fungi, wildlife, domestic animals, and other small creatures. Large areas of forest that took hundreds of years to grow have been destroyed by insects and disease.

12.2 FOREST TREE INSECTS

Insects that can injure or, if not kept under control, destroy stands of trees exist in eight classes, as follows:

Figure 12-1. Entomologist collecting elm spanworms from defoliated limb of a northern red oak. Worms indicated by arrows. (Courtesy USDA Forest Service)

1. The *defoliators*, chewing insects that destroy or injure the foliage of coniferous and deciduous trees by stripping them of their leaves, which causes food production to stop. The tree becomes weakened and may die if leaf damage continues. Figure 12-1 shows a forester collecting elm spanworm specimens.

2. *Wood borers*, chewing insects with mouth parts that bore into the sapwood and heartwood of branches or attack stems and roots, which makes the wood less useful for commercial purposes.

3. *Sucking insects* have mouth parts that can penetrate tissues, enabling the insect to suck fluid from a tree. These are mostly aphids and scales. They rarely kill the tree but damage it to the extent of slowing its growth. An exception is the balsam wooly aphid, which is deadly to the balsam firs.

4. *Gall makers*, insects that cause swellings on leaves or twigs or on the bark of the main stem. These are mostly wasps, aphids, gnats, and midges, which seldom kill trees but cause deformity.

5. *Bark beetles*, insects with chewing mouth parts that attack the stem of a tree. The larvae and adults of the *Scolytidae* burrow into the phloem, eating into the soft tissue and the tree is killed by girdling.

6. *Terminal feeders*, insects that feed in the tips of the twigs, buds, and shoots, distorting growth and causing tree deformity, which affects timber value. Repeated tip damage results in tree death.

7. *Root feeders,* mostly beetle larvae called white grubs and wire worms. Some feed also on the bark of seedlings.

8. *Seed insects*, which deposit eggs within developing cones. The larvae feed unnoticed, destroying the seeds or nuts; mostly larvae of moths, wasps, and beetles.

Bark beetles are the most destructive of all forest insects, even though they are quite small, the largest being hardly over ⅜ inch (1 centimeter) in length. Figure 12-2 is a picture of a Southern pine bark beetle magnified many times. During one outbreak of the Western pine bark beetle, over 1 billion board feet of ponderosa pine timber were destroyed in California. In the early 1900s the larch sawfly, a defoliating insect, destroyed the mature larch throughout its entire range. Millions of cords of spruce and balsam were destroyed by the spruce budworm in eastern America in the 1910s. In the 1930s, the Canadian government estimated their loss of timber through attack by insects to be seven times as great as the loss by fire.

Hardy and strong though they may seem, trees are constantly engaged in a battle of survival with their insect enemies. Not only are they under ceaseless attack by insects, but the tree seeds are eaten as well by insects. Planted seeds are infested by soil insects. The roots of seedlings are often destroyed by insects. Until the

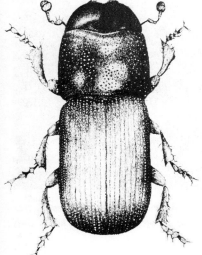

Figure 12-2. Southern pine bark beetle, shown many times its normal size. (Courtesy of USDA Forest Service)

final tree crops are ready for cutting, they are under attack. After having been cut into logs, they still are subject to attack while awaiting transportation in the woods. A number of insects attack the seasoned or partly seasoned lumber at the lumber mill. Even the finished wood product is threatened by termites or by powder post beetles. The attack of insects upon all forest resources costs hundreds of millions of dollars annually in wasted wood products. In addition, vast expenditures for insect control—applications and research—raise the costs even higher.

12.3 METHODS OF INSECT CONTROL

Natural control of injurious insects takes place through climatic conditions, parasites, predators, disease, rodents, and birds. Rearing parasites and predators and releasing them in a region of insect outbreak is called *biological* control. Nature produces insect mortality by means of high and low temperatures and through extreme drought or moisture. Through special methods of log piling and brush disposal, people can also help nature control insects.

Special forest practices and in rare cases the use of insecticides are two forms of insect control (see Figure 12-3). Insect damage can

Figure 12-3. Power-spraying insecticide on Southern pine beetle infested trees in South Carolina. Tractor is equipped with tanks and pump. (Courtesy USDA Forest Service)

be prevented to some extent by proper management and silviculture practices. It is difficult to use and apply insecticides under normal forest conditions, but spraying from low-flying planes seems to be an effective practice in the few situations where controls are possible and the benefits justify the cost.

Most of the damage from insects takes place during the insect's growth (developing) period and some species produce several generations a year. Most insects have a life cycle that includes *metamorphosis* or complete transformation in form between the juvenile and adult stages. For example, a caterpillar becomes a butterfly. For one group of insects, the eggs hatch into larvae, developing into caterpillars that feed on trees. The caterpillars when fully developed go through a resting stage during which they form cocoons and change into pupae. After a period of being pupae, they undergo metamorphosis and become adults.

Where defoliator insects are epidemic, the forest appears to look brownish and unnatural at a distance. Large quantities of insect droppings on the ground are a good indication that insects are at work. Boring insects can be found where a fine wood powder called *frass* is seen at the base of the tree. Where there is tip moth damage, new growing leaders bend and shrivel up or turn reddish brown and die.

The natural elements play a big part in helping trees fight off insect attacks. A good freeze, for example, can help. On the other hand, a tree's resistance to bark-beetle attack is lowered by drought. Then, too, a flood or excess rain can weaken trees just as insect attack does.

Table 12–1 lists some common tree insects, the damage they can do, and how they may be controlled.

12.4 FOREST TREE DISEASES

Trees, like people, are vulnerable to many diseases. Like people, trees are attacked in various places by different kinds of diseases. *Forest pathology* is the study of diseases of trees. Some foes work on the main body trunk, some on the roots, and some on the leaves. Vigorous trees are attacked less by diseases. The older, weak trees or young seedlings that are struggling to become established trees are the most susceptible. If a forest is managed correctly, seldom will disease be serious enough to require overt control. Well-managed forests are healthy and comparatively devoid of disease.

TABLE 12-1

Principal Tree-Damaging Insects and Methods of Control. (Data Courtesy USDA Forestry Science Laboratory, Research Triangle Park, N.C.)

Insect	Nature of Damage	Control
Gypsy moth	Defoliation	Insecticide[1]
Bark beetle	Kills trees by girdling cambium layer and phloem	Fell; salvage merchantable stems; peel bark or use insecticide[a]
Sawflies	Defoliates, reduces growth; individuals or groups of trees may be killed	Insecticide[1]
White pine weevil	Kills leaders and thus produces forked and crooked boles	Insecticide[1]
Scales and aphids	Sucking insects stunt growth	Insecticide[1]
Pales weevil	Girdles seedlings	Insecticide[a]

[1]Consult forester or county agricultural agent on which insecticide to use and how to apply it.

Tree diseases are of two main types: nonparasitic and parasitic, often called environmental and organic. The nonparasitic diseases are caused by drought, sunscald, winter injury as from heavy ice storms and snow, improper nutrition of the trees, air pollution by smoke and gases, flooding, and soil pollution. The salt laid on highways during winter months pollutes the nearby soil and in some instances kills trees. Ocean spray, which feels so good on one's face, is a prime cause of disease in the coastal areas. This sea spray can be blown inland by hurricanes and result in tree damage far from the coast.

The parasitic diseases are caused by organisms that live within various parts of the tree and take nutrients from it while contributing nothing to the well-being of the tree. There are five groups of such organisms: viruses, bacteria, nematodes, mistletoes, and fungi.

Viruses cause minor galls, a condition known as witches-broom, and the serious phloem necrosis in elms and locusts. A number of bacteria that are involved in many serious diseases of agricultural plants are of little importance in forest trees. Nematodes, a group of parasitic worms, can be a problem for tree seedlings. Mistletoes, parasitic seed-bearing plants, are widespread and cause serious damage, the dwarf mistletoe of the West in particular. The most important cause of tree disease are the parasitic fungi. Saprophytic fungi decay dead trees and are important in the recycling of nutrients within the forest ecosystem. The parasitic fungi attack living trees and are a serious problem in all forest regions. Considerably more timber is lost annually to fungal diseases than is lost to fire.

The life cycle of a typical fungus consists of two basic stages, the vegetative and the reproductive. The vegetative stage begins with the germination of a spore, the fungal equivalent of a seed. Out of the spore grows a microscopically fine hollow filament called a *hypha*, which penetrates into wood or foliage and grows very rapidly, branching and rebranching to produce a gossamer, interwoven network known as a *mycelium*. These mycelia dissolve the tree's cell walls and convert them and the contents of the cell into food. The second stage is the reproductive stage in which *hyphae* grow to the surface and produce fruiting bodies, which split and release spores to be carried away by the wind. The form, texture, color, and location of these fruiting bodies are how most fungi are recognized. Familiar examples are mushrooms and conks.

For convenience the fungal diseases can be sorted into three large groups: the foliage diseases, the stem diseases, and the rotting diseases. Although widespread and of great importance in horticulture, foliage diseases are a problem in forest trees only in that they can reduce the rate of growth of the infected trees.

Stem diseases can in turn be broken into three groups, the cankers, the rusts, and the wilts. Among these are the epidemic diseases, which can result in rapid and widespread loss of forest trees.

The chestnut blight is an example of a stem canker disease. The American chestnut once was one of the most important and useful eastern trees. Very widespread, it often accounted for as much as one half of the trees in many forest stands. The fungus was introduced into New York probably prior to 1900 on imported Chinese chestnuts, and the native species had no resistance. The windblown spores from an infected tree could travel great distances to enter tiny cracks or breaks in the bark of other chestnuts. The stem is killed by girdling as the cambium is destroyed. By 1950 a living noninfected chestnut tree was a rarity. Today the American chestnut is no longer a viable species. The potential threat of similar epidemics of exotic disease to other native species is a source of anxiety for many foresters.

The Dutch elm disease is an example of the wilt disease. This fungus, probably native to the Orient, was introduced into this country from Europe around 1930. The disease is spread by the elm bark beetle, which upon emerging from an infected tree is covered with spores. When the insect burrows under the bark of an uninfected tree, it is effectively inoculated. The fungus grows rapidly within the vascular tissue of the elm, and death is caused by physical blocking of the movement of moisture and nutrients to the foliage and perhaps by the production of a poison that kills living cells. The spread of this disease has been rapid. Many feel that the future of elms, particularly in the northern states, is in jeopardy.

There are a number of serious rusts of fruit trees. White pine blister rust and the fusiform rusts of the southern pines are the most important. These rusts have an unusual and complex life cycle involving the infection of two widely different species of plants known as alternate hosts and the production of more than one type of spore. The fungus moves from one host, species A, to a second host, species B, and then back to species A again.

White pine blister rust, another disease introduced from Europe, is an extremely destructive disease of eastern and western white pines and of sugar pine of California and Oregon. Simply put, the disease is spread by the movement of spores from infected currant or gooseberry bushes to the needles of the pines. The fungus moves from the needles into the phloem and cambium of limbs and stem. The name is from the orange-yellow spore-filled blisters formed on the bark. Whenever infection reaches the main stem the tree is doomed, for destruction of the phloem continues until the stem, no matter how large, is girdled. Infection can be severe and often entire stands are killed.

The southern fusiform rust, which infects a number of the southern pines, has as its alternate host any of the numerous red oak species of the region. While not as destructive as the white pine blister rust, this disease is of increasing concern to forest managers. It is most virulent on loblolly pine, which is being intensively managed with costly site preparation and fertilization.

The rotting fungi, while they rarely cause death directly, are responsible for rendering great volumes of wood worthless. There are two major types, the root-decaying fungi and the heart-rotting fungi. The *Fomes* root rots typify the first category. Though they attack a variety of species, they are most troublesome in eastern white pine and in plantations of the southern pines. Working in the roots and butt of the tree, they weaken the tree, making it susceptible to windthrow, and reduce its growth (Figure 12-4). The heart-rotting fungi destroy the nonliving heartwood of the tree and, aside from leaving it mechanically weaker, do not otherwise influence its health and vigor (Figure 12-5). The rotten wood is of course valueless. Spores of the heart-rotting fungi must enter through breaks in

Figure 12-4. (*Left*) Butt rot in a hardwood tree split open to expose center of log. (Courtesy USDA Forest Service)

Figure 12-5. (*Right*) Heartrot at center of a tree makes it more susceptible to breakage from wind and ice. (Courtesy USDA Forest Service)

the bark. Once they have germinated, the disease develops very slowly, and rot is rarely a problem in young stands. In the old-growth conifer forests of the West, a 50 to 60 percent loss of volume to rot is not uncommon.

12.5 CONTROL OF TREE DISEASES

While there are direct, chemical, control measures for use in orna-mental and orchard trees, these are not feasible in forest situations. The forester must rely on indirect means of reducing losses caused by disease. Through proper management, vigorous and healthy stands may be maintained. The impact of many of the rotting fungi can be held at acceptable levels by reducing the amount of bark and root breakage to deny the fungi entrance and by planning to harvest at an age before rot has become serious. Rusts can be controlled by the reduction of alternate hosts. This approach was followed for years in the western white pine region, and thousands of high school and forestry students have spent the summer grubbing up gooseberry bushes in the western mountains.

The seedlings of longleaf pine in the southern coastal plane when infected with the brown spot disease cannot grow and remain arrested in the seedling stage for decades. A low-intensity prescribed fire destroys the disease while doing no harm to the fire-resistant seedlings.

Cutting and removal of diseased trees as soon as the infection is noticed reduces the source of infection for healthy trees. This is the recommended action against Dutch elm disease and oak wilt in forest situations.

Fomes root disease can enter the freshly cut stumps created by thinning a young stand. The fungus moves down into the roots of the stumps and into the remaining trees through the soil and root grafts. Dusting the stump with borax or applying the spores of a saprophitic fungus can deny entrance to the *Fomes* fungus.

Last, and perhaps most promising, is the increasing success of the forest geneticist in breeding trees that are resistant to specific diseases. Some success has already been achieved against white pine blister rust in western white pine, against southern fusiform rust in loblolly pine, and against Dutch elm disease. Much work has been devoted to developing hybrids of American chestnut that are resistant to its blight.

12.6 SUMMARY

Insects, diseases, natural disasters, and human-caused problems can rake complete forests. Insects and diseases usually can be kept under control through careful forest management and proper treatments.

Insects that produce damage in forests can be classified into eight categories, of which beetles are the most destructive. Damaging insects are controlled through natural factors and by foresters through spraying and burning infested biomaterial. The killing of insects by other organisms is referred to as biological control.

Nonparasitic tree diseases are those caused by natural events. Parasitic diseases are those caused by pathogens. Widely known parasitic diseases are chestnut blight, white pine blister rust, and Dutch elm disease. Control is difficult; therefore, forests must be managed to reduce the losses. Natural control takes place through weather conditions and through parasites and predators such as rodents and birds. In some cases insecticides are effective, but they are expensive to purchase and apply.

chapter 13

Damage by Weather, Catastrophic Action, and Animals

13.1 WEATHER AS AN ENEMY OF THE FOREST

While insects, diseases, fires, and some animals can damage or destroy a forest, climatic conditions can also do considerable harm. Forests are able to cope with weather conditions normal for their region but can be injured by the abnormal. Exceptionally heavy ice and snow bend and break branches and trunks of trees. Lightning damages and kills trees by splitting their trunks and knocking off bark and limbs. Long droughts may cause trees to die from lack of water. Floods also cause damage by undermining trees, washing out dirt from around the roots, softening the soil and causing trees to fall, and, most importantly, suffocating the roots by reducing available oxygen. However, such actions usually are not extensive, injuring or destroying only some of the trees. It is weather quite abnormal for a particular forest that results in major damage, such as a hurricane.

13.2 DROUGHT AND HIGH TEMPERATURES

If a region is subject to prolonged dry spells, drought-resistant species or specially bred genetic *cultivars* may be planted. It would also be wise to get rid of all undesirable woody brush species that will compete for soil moisture with the desired trees. Usually, irrigation of a forest is too costly, but the watering of shelterbelt plantings may be worthwhile.

Sometimes high temperatures can cause severe mortality of tree seedlings. Nurseries make special provisions to provide partial shade and water for certain hardwoods and coniferous seedlings during periods of intense heat. Tree mortality caused by heat usually happens in places where movement of the air is poor. The air temperature must rise to 120 to 130°F (49 to 54°C) for healthy plantings to be killed.

Sunscald is the permanent wilting of young leaves, and it occurs in the summer when temperatures are high and soil moisture supply is low. It also occurs during the summer to southern trees that have thin bark. This is the result of cambium tissue being overheated by solar radiation.

13.3 FROST ACTION

Young trees may be pushed from the ground by frost action (heaving) of wet, clay soil. As the water expands upon freezing, it moves upward carrying soil particles and tree roots with it. The trees can be lifted so far out of the ground that the roots are exposed and die by desiccation (drying out). Small trees and seedlings are so susceptible to being killed by frost or drought that it is necessary in some instances to plant trees that are 2 years old to be sure they are hardy enough to survive. Late spring frosts are particularly damaging to trees after the buds have opened and growth of foliage has started.

Warm, clear days during the winter while the ground is still frozen may bring *winter foliage burning*. The moisture lost by rapid transpiration cannot be replaced by the roots in partially frozen soil, causing browning and killing of needles. *Winterkill* is a condition caused by sudden rapid freezing of cambium tissue that has been thawed by a brief period of high radiant heating during winter.

13.4 DAMAGE BY WIND, RAIN, SNOW, AND ICE

Trees can be uprooted and overturned by high winds. Tops of trees may be broken off by moderate winds. Tornados, as they sweep through forests, can level swaths of trees. Hurricanes also severely

Figure 13-1. Tangled mass of loblolly pine trees damaged by a high wind storm. (Courtesy USDA Forest Service)

damage forests. Figure 13-1 shows what was once a showpiece forest that became a tangled mass of trees in a windstorm.

Proper planning to maintain correct density of trees can help reduce wind damage to a forest. Maintaining good borders of shrubs and small trees at edges of the forest can help stop the wind from sweeping through the stand with subsequent desiccation or possible breakage of limbs or treetops.

Heavy rains can result in flooding, land slippage, gullying, and overland flow of water that erodes the soil from the roots of trees. In most of our forests, the soil stays sufficiently porous so that rainwater can soak into the soil without surface flow, and there is no erosion. In the high mountains, forests can be damaged by snowslides and avalanches. Keeping vegetation growing on the upper slopes helps in reducing snowslides to some extent. Leaves can be stripped from trees by heavy hail. Hailstorms usually are of a local nature and do not affect whole forests. Such storms usually are not disastrous because leaves will grow again on the trees and the damage is not often permanent.

Heavy, wet snow and freezing rains pile upon tree tops and the extra weight breaks the crowns. This allows fungi to enter the trees, with resultant decay. Nature produces many magnificent scenes during the changing seasons, but it also can do damage that is not quickly repaired.

Usually, trees are planted in areas where they are adapted to the normal weather. Trees planted out of their natural habitat are the ones most likely to be damaged by ice or snow. Hardwoods are frequently damaged by ice, while conifers are additionally hurt by wet, heavy snow. Trees that have narrow crowns of short perpendicular branches can resist damage from ice and heavy snow better than do those with wide, full crowns, because of smaller area for the ice and snow to accumulate on and because any accumulation slides off more easily.

13.5 DAMAGE FROM EARTHQUAKES, VOLCANOES, AND TSUNAMI

In some local areas a catastrophe may result from an earthquake. In 1959 a severe earthquake occurred in the upper Madison River Valley of Idaho. Hegben Lake was tilted because of the extensive faulting that resulted from the earthquake; new land was created and other land was inundated. Streams in the forest were diverted and falling boulders crashed down on the trees, breaking and killing them. A huge slide sent trees, boulders, and earth cascading into the Madison River Canyon, which created a natural dam almost 500 feet high. A lake formed behind the dam and killed the trees flooded by the water backed over them. Reelfoot Lake in northwest Tennessee was formed following the subsidence of several thousand acres caused by an earthquake in 1811.

An earthquake, while doing damage in its local area, may also cause tsunami (tidal waves) thousands of miles away on a far seacoast. Trees in low-lying parts of these coasts may be damaged or felled because of the large amount of water that flows around them and washes them out.

An erupting volcano may cause local devastation, and the ashes can also result in widespread damage. A flow of lava destroyed large areas of trees in the Mount Katmai eruption in Alaska in 1912.

Thousands of acres of forest were buried in the hot lava flow, killing the tree growth. Fine ash from this eruption was carried great distances by winds, causing minor damage to foliage and trees. Fine ash, blast effect, and fire destroyed vast areas of prime forest on the slopes of Mount Saint Helens in Washington when it erupted in 1980.

13.6 SMOG AND OTHER AIR POLLUTION

Smog, defined as a fog made denser by smoke or chemical fumes or other air pollutants, not only causes damage to peoples' lungs but also to forests growing near a smog area. Southern California has experienced tree damage, particularly in the Los Angeles region. Healthy branches and green leaves take on a brownish color because of tissue damage from the pollutants, and death is a frequent result.

In Tennessee where copper mines are located, in the past, uncontrolled smelter fumes containing sulfur dioxide (SO_2) killed trees and all vegetation for distances of 8 miles (13 kilometers) from the smelters. Sulfur dioxide reacts with water (H_2O) to produce sulfurous acid (H_2SO_3).

Emission of large quantities of particulate and gases results from coal-burning electric power plants and chemical industries. These materials may damage forests locally or travel thousands of miles before being deposited as dry fallout or in precipitation (rain). Records show that rain in the eastern United States has become more acid in the last 20 years as a result of increased industrialization. Acid rain has not seriously damaged trees, but fish production has decreased in some streams and lakes in the Northeast.

13.7 DAMAGE BY ANIMALS

Our forests have long been the natural home and refuge for many game and fur-bearing animals. The lower branches of trees, shrubs, and vines (such as honeysuckle) of the forests have also provided forage (food) for domestic animals. As an animal population increases, so does its need for food. Trees and other vegetation in some instances are damaged in the animals' struggle for survival.

Domestic grazing animals can retard natural reproduction of forests by compacting the soil by trampling. They injure the ground cover and cause the surface of the ground to become exposed and compacted; hence, erosion can take place. Of all the domestic animals that do damage to forests, hogs are among the worst because they burrow into the ground and eat the tender, nutritious roots of many young, growing trees.

Among wildlife, larger mammals such as deer and moose cause extensive forest damage. They are beautiful and fascinating to watch, with their big sloe eyes and regal antlers, but they can do damage. In the Lake Superior area, moose have formed browse lines as high as 11 feet from the ground in satisfying their hunger. Reproduction of trees in some western states has been seriously impaired by overbrowsing elk. Overbrowsing in most cases is the result of overpopulation.

Deer have actually eliminated all palatable growth in some forest areas by overbrowsing. In some forests no trees under 30 years of age can be found as a result of deer overbrowsing. Where deer are too abundant, entire acorn crops of some oak forests have been consumed, preventing these oaks from reproducing. Nipping off the leaders of young trees is a favorite habit of deer. They also rub the velvet from their antlers against trees, thus removing the bark that serves as protection. Browsing damage is greatest where herds of deer are confined to small areas, as is the case in the northern states and in the Rocky Mountains during deep winter snows.

In the Pacific Coast region, second-growth timber is being damaged or killed by the black bear. The bear exposes the juicy cambium near the base of certain trees by scratching and biting off the tree's outer bark in the spring and early summer. It has been determined through analysis of a bear's stomach that cambium is a major food item. On the Olympic Peninsula of Washington, bears have killed as many as 40 trees per acre by girdling. The bear's favorite tree is the Douglas fir. Sap-licking damage is done to the western hemlock, the Sitka spruce, and the western red cedar.

Rabbits also are among the damagers of forests. They nip and nibble the young shoots of trees, and this results in a deformed bush of a tree, if it survives at all. Because of the short reproduction cycle of the rabbit, it quickly overpopulates its habitat and damages forest vegetation. Many control methods have been tried, for example, fencing small areas in tree nurseries, but these clever animals usually seem to find a way to get under or around the fences. Major success has been experienced with repellents.

The porcupine is a troublesome rodent. It kills or damages trees quite extensively, particularly in the Pacific Northwest. Its favorite food in the West is the bark of ponderosa and lodgepole pine. In the Great Lakes states and in New England its favorite foods are the northern hardwoods. These animals do not hibernate, so they girdle trees all year long. Much of the wood is exposed to further attack by insects and disease, if the girdling does not kill the tree outright. Porcupines will select the healthiest and most vigorous trees instead of the poorest trees in the stand. In New York State, a bounty was offered in 1908 because of the damage they were doing to trees. Each year, this animal is becoming a greater menace in Oregon and southwestern Washington. Thousands have been trapped each year in Oregon, and game hunters are requested to shoot these animals when they see them. Porcupines have been increasing in numbers since the wildfires that formerly destroyed them and kept them to a minimum have been reduced.

Beavers, flat-tailed animals that can build whole cities under water through the felling of small pole-sized trees (animal engineers about whom Walt Disney has made a motion picture), are said to have damaged more trees than all other species of animals combined. They cut down trees for their food, housing, and dam construction. The best control of beaver is by trapping, although in most states the animal is protected. Special licenses are issued for beaver trappers, and only a limited number may be caught each year.

Squirrels, chipmunks, and white-footed mice do widespread damage to seed crops. Seed crop loss from the squirrels is serious, but control measures are seldom undertaken. In southern Michigan, where winter icing is severe, tree squirrels have been seen stripping the younger bark from sugar maples in hardwood forests because they could not get to their acorn caches. One of the preferred foods of the white-footed mice is tree seed. They can destroy most of an entire seed crop of a given species, but they can be controlled. Rodents are cunning animals and survive even when exposed to bait seed treated with poison. The repellents used today actually train mice to change their eating habits. If a mouse finds the treated seed not to his taste, often it will look for something else to eat.

Domestic sheep grazing in the national forests of the Southwest is harmful to ponderosa pine reproduction. During the early summer dry period, the sheep will satisfy their thirst by browsing on the succulent roots of young pines. Not only do they damage the trees, but as a result of large numbers of animals trampling down the grassy areas, the ground becomes exposed, compacted, and subject to erosion. The trees' roots are exposed to desiccation, abrasion, and disease. By carefully regulating the number of domestic animals that graze in the national forests, the destruction has been kept under control.

In Africa, elephants cause the most spectacular damage seen

anywhere in the world. To get at foliage and twigs they will push over, break, and uproot trees. Those they cannot push over they debark and delimb. Large areas of forests have been changed in shape and size by these large herbivores. Because of extensive wildlife hunting and watching, the growth of trees has been considered to be of secondary importance by the authorities, since wildlife brings people to the area and supports the economy.

Not all animal life is detrimental to the welfare of the forest. Birds are very helpful in keeping down insect populations. The woodpecker is extremely important to the life of the forest and has been known to kill practically the entire brood of spruce beetles in some areas.

That social outcast, the skunk, has been responsible for consuming 14,520 grubs per acre over an 8-acre tract in Manitoba, Canada. Poor sites of land have been cultivated by the burrowing action of many small animals. Beneficial effects of grazing have been observed in the pine forests of the South and in open conifer forests of the West where grazing has been properly regulated. Grass, when dried, becomes a serious fire hazard. Unwanted hardwoods have been eliminated in an area being reproduced to conifers by browsing sheep and goats.

13.8 CONTROL OF WILDLIFE

Control of damage to forest by wildlife is in the province of good wildlife management combined with proper forest management. During those times of the year when food is least plentiful, the wildlife population is likely to be the most destructive because they are trying to survive by eating whatever they can find. They are not interested in the effects they are producing on the trees in the forest. They will eat whatever is available, whether it is tree bark, exposed roots, or tasty leaders.

Many people in the United States oppose the hunting of animals. Yet, though the effect is minimal, hunting does have some bearing on the control of wildlife. Animals suffer, starve, or become diseased when food is not available. It is perhaps preferable to destroy an animal by one quick shot than to expose it to weeks of hunger until it is so weak that it dies or is eaten by other animals in the forest, which are also hungry.

Other methods of control are being tried, but there are few reports of success. Fences have been used to control animals, but building them involves prohibitive costs. Trapping and transporting live animals to other areas has been tried but has not reduced populations significantly, for wildlife tends to be very prolific. Predators, disease, and starvation are the ways through which nature takes care to reduce populations of wildlife. Survival of the fittest appears to be the true way of wildlife.

The type of wildlife found in any region is determined by the kind of food, cover, and water available in the forest for these animals to live on. Clear, cool streams are the preferred home for most game fish, such as trout that live in the forest watersheds. (Catfish appear to prefer muddy water.) Beaver and ducks require water for their homes. The forest supplies water for such species from springs and lake runoffs, streams, and swamps. When a wide area has been destructively cut or burnt, this abruptly changes the wildlife habitat, and for many years the balance of nature is disturbed. Species of animals favored by the earlier forest condition are reduced in number, while species favored by the new condition increase in number.

State laws govern hunting and fishing partly in order that the balance of nature can be kept. To preserve the balance and to avoid changing the habitats and the supply of animals, only limited amounts of certain animals and fish may be taken from the forests. Wildlife managers and foresters work hand in hand in controlling the forest land and the animals. They are well acquainted with the laws governing hunting, trapping, and fishing. They have studied both wildlife management and forest protection, and each stays aware of current developments in the field of the other.

Intelligent planning includes studying the needs of animals and birds and the development of practices that will improve the forest for wildlife while at the same time protecting the forest crop from the wildlife. Timing is among the important factors involved. The following are some of the current management practices:

1. Where there is an abundance of deer, logging, stand improvement, or thinning may be scheduled for mid or late winter, when the animals are most in need of food, in order to make available browse from tops and limbs when food cannot be found elsewhere.

2. Where there are long distances between sources of water, wildlife managers find it beneficial to build small ponds to hold back seepage or runoff water from slopes. This has the effect of spreading the wildlife out over the forest and increases the effective range for many species; the larger ponds can be used by waterfowl.

3. Planting game food mixtures along logging roads and in planned patches increases the food supply and improves hunting of ruffed grouse.

4. In a badly burned northern forest, distribution of a few old hollow logs near low spots is a means of encouraging ruffed grouse to spread out during the mating season.

5. The food supply of many small animals and birds is increased by clearing out small openings in the forest during logging and planting berry-bearing shrubs and legumes.

6. The fencing of farm woodlots excludes livestock and prevents their taking wildlife food and trampling down the brush and shrubs needed as cover by many species.

7. Placing rock or log deflectors in small streams permits the current to cut pools deeper than the normal stream bed and makes better fish habitats.

13.9 SUMMARY

Forests can suffer damage from adverse weather conditions (drought or flood, cold or heat, snow and ice, winds), from catastrophies (lightning, earthquakes, volcanic eruptions, tsunamis), from air pollution, and from animals (certain wildlife and domestic species).

Weather damage is minimal if the stand is of a species appropriate for the location, if the stand is neither too dense nor too sparse, and if steps are taken to assure an adequate supply of moisture.

Wildlife species that damage forests include deer, moose, black bears, porcupines, beaver, rabbits, squirrels, chipmunks, and white-footed mice. Domestic animals harmful to forests through tree damage and trampling of the ground are hogs, sheep, and cattle, unless kept to limited numbers. Birds, however, often are helpful by killing off insects. Some animal life helps a forest through consumption of tree-damaging grubs and the eating of shrubs that could otherwise become a fire hazard or compete with the forest timber crop.

The balance of nature is maintained in forests largely through natural means. Where this balance is disrupted by the actions of people, game laws and intelligent land management practices must be used by both wildlife and forest managers to reduce the adverse effects of this imbalance.

chapter 14

Fire Management

> *The most widespread forestry practice in the United States, and in many ways the most important and effective historically, is organized protection against wildfire.*[1]

14.1 FIRE AND THE FOREST

Wildfires, one of which is shown in Figure 14-1, cut a wide path of ruin through our nation's forests each year, destroying seed and young trees. Older trees often are damaged and in many instances killed. Large fire wounds on some trees invite attacks by insects and disease, resulting in tree death years later. If the trees survive the ordeal of a fire, they often are left with ugly scars and serious decay, which mar the lumber and reduce its value.

Yet many of our most valuable forests exist today because of past wildfires. The pioneer species that compose them seeded the burned area to create new and vigourous forests. Many species of trees, particularly among the conifers, have evolved, largely through the development of thick insulating bark, a tolerance to low-intensity fire. Others, such as some of the very intolerant pioneer species and

---

[1]G. W. Sharpe, G. W. Hendee, and S. W. Allen, *Introduction to Forestry*, 4th ed. (New York: McGraw-Hill Book Company, 1976), p. 325.

Figure 14-1. A wildfire in a young pine forest. Fires can get out of control when sudden windshifts occur. (Courtesy USDA Forest Service)

those with serotinous cones, have developed a dependence upon fire for their effective regeneration. Even the animal life of certain forest types has evolved to benefit from low-intensity fires. The vegetational change following such fires creates a greater volume of some nutritious foods, and increased cover. For such evolutionary change to have occurred, forest fires must have been taking place in these timber types long before humans entered the picture. Indeed, there are many indications that this is true. Fires should therefore be conceived as part of the natural long-range scheme of things. It is perhaps only where the timing and the intensity of a fire disrupts peoples' plans and activities that fire should be considered as totally undesirable.

Recognition of this dual good and bad nature of fire in the forest has led to its use as a beneficial tool in forestry. When used in a controlled or prescribed manner, fire has a number of uses. Unwanted vegetation growing beneath fire-resistant species of trees can be controlled or eliminated. Grasses, seeds, and browse for wildlife use can be increased. Certain diseases, such as the brown spot disease of longleaf pine, can be controlled. Proper seedbed conditions can be created for natural regeneration of a new forest. Heavy accumulations of logging slash, which hinder movement within a logged area and its eventual regeneration, can be reduced. However, perhaps the most important and profitable use of prescribed fire is what are known as hazard reduction burns. As a stand ages, the available fuel, an accumulation of litter, grasses, dead twigs, limbs, and brush, increases. By carefully choosing the season of year and weather conditions, a pine stand may be burned with a low-intensity fire that consumes only a portion of the available fuel. This ensures that for many years any wildfire that might burn the area will be of low intensity with few adverse effects.

The growing use of prescribed fire requires that the term forest fire be thought of more precisely as either "wildfire" or "prescribed fire" and has created the modern concept of fire management, a strategic part of land management.

Environmental impacts of prescribed burning are limited at any given time to a small percentage of the total forest area. Nevertheless, there are problems and risks. The escape of a prescribed fire from control is a continual risk. Although wood smoke contains little if any of the oxides of nitrogen and sulfur, two of our most serious air pollutants, it does contain large amounts of ash and hydrocarbon products of incomplete combustion. These are known collectively as particulate matter and can contribute much to air pollution. Regulations to control the amount of prescribed burning done at one time and the air quality conditions under which it may be done have been created in most states where prescribed fire is widely employed. The new field of smoke management is directed at minimizing the impact of forest fire smoke upon our atmosphere. Factors that influence the quantity and quality of smoke and its potential impact are atmospheric stability, fuel volumes, types and moisture content, the type of fire (heading with or against the wind), and the nearness of smoke-sensitive areas such as cities, airports, or busy highways.

It should be emphasized that fire is not useful in all forest types. Most hardwood forests and the thin-barked spruces and fires of the northern forest should not be burned. No forest type, except longleaf pine, can tolerate even light fires when they are very young. Prescribed burning on easily eroded soils and within many watersheds is rarely beneficial.

The use of fire, fire management, and smoke management are of recent origin, however, and our overriding image of fire in the forests tends still to come from the past history of wildfires.

14.2 HISTORIC SIGNIFICANCE OF WILDFIRES

Even though people have been burning the woods for their own gain since prehistory, the fear of raging forest fires is well founded. Descriptive allegories of poets and prophets of Biblical times indicate that the havoc produced by range and forest fires was well known to the ancients. Germany enacted ordinances against fire as early as the latter part of the sixteenth century. California's giant sequoias bear scars from forest fires that took place in the year 245 A.D.

Historically, forest fires have been infrequent in tropical rain forests or in deciduous broad-leaved forests of the temperate zones. On the other hand, coniferous forests and the evergreen broad-leaved species of hot, dry, zones develop conditions that are ideally suited for spreading fire. In essence, fire spreads rapidly when both the air and fuel are dry, and the fuel is in loose layers allowing for free flow of air, combustion gases, and smoke. Thus, on clear, sunny days, with low atmospheric humidity and steady winds, wildfires may travel downwind at speeds of 10 miles per hour or faster, while spreading less fast in lateral directions from the ignition point.

In coniferous forests the fallen twigs, branches, and tops (slash), plus the resinous needles both living and dead, make excellent fuel for fires. Examples of forests with evergreen broad-leaved species are found in the chaparral forest of California and the eucalyptus forests of Australia. These provide an ideal fuel because the leaves of these species contain flammable waxes and oils that burn fiercely when ignited, even when green. Many consider the wind to be the most important shaper of a forest fire. Even heavily compacted and sometimes wet fuels may burn when there are strong winds. Strong winds have been the major cause of some of our worst wildfires. We will here discuss two such disastrous wildfires.

After a considerably lengthy dry period in 1825, at 1 P.M. on the windy afternoon of October 7, the Miramichi fire began. It started about 60 miles (96 kilometers) above Newcastle in New Brunswick, Canada, on the Miramichi River. Nine hours later, pushed by gusty winds and fed by millions of coniferous trees, it had burned an area 80 miles (130 kilometers) long and 25 miles (40 kilometers) wide, or slightly more than 1.3 million acres. In the wake of the fire, 160 people were confirmed to have died, and many buildings were destroyed.

On Sunday morning, October 8, 1871, the northern Wisconsin logging village of Peshtigo, which had provided lumber for the rising young city of Chicago, fell victim to the worst wildfire in American history. Fires started earlier by men burning slash on the North-western Railroad were combined by high winds, causing loss of control. This happened after a dry winter, spring, and summer.

By noon of that Sunday the smoke had become so intense from the fire raging toward Peshtigo that the sun was totally obliterated above the logging village. By nightfall, flame began to fall into the sawdust streets and the board sidewalks burst into flames. Houses were literally exploding into flames. The heat from the millions of burning pine trees was so intense that the survivors, who had jumped into the Peshtigo River to escape the heat, were quoted as saying that the surface water was nearly boiling. Some of the victims of the fire were actually cremated before they could get out of their homes. Crates of new axe heads melted and fused together. The final count of fatalities amounted to 1,500 people.

Ironically, on this same day the great Chicago fire took place, claiming the lives of 200 people. Fires burned the telegraph wires from Peshtigo before the Peshtigo fire struck, and thus it was over a month before the United States knew what had happened at the head of Lake Michigan. For this reason no sudden impact of horror reached the public, and therefore our worst wildfire, in terms of human suffering, is hardly known today.

The two wildfires just discussed may be classed as "blowup" fires, fires that suddenly increase with such intensity or rate, because of the availability of fuel and/or strong winds, that their spread is so rapid that no form of direct control is sufficient to stop them. Also, any fire plans made earlier are usually upset. Fires of this type reportedly have become so intense almost instantly that windstorms of near cyclonic proportions, windstorms with violent whirling air movement, take place at their centers.

Blowup fires, or high-intensity fires as the fire physicist calls them, have been studied for a number of years, and while we still need more knowledge, certain features appear to be common to most such dangerous fires. Most of what is known can be related to fuel and wind. A high-intensity fire requires a large volume of fuel of such individual particle size and moisture content that it can burn completely—release all its energy—in synchronization with the forward movement of the fire. Second, wind speed must decrease as altitude decreases. This permits the development of a strong convection column or "chimney" of smoke and hot gases directly above the fire. The energy moving upward into this towering convection column may exceed the energy of surface winds, and the fire begins to create the powerful winds (updraft winds) mentioned earlier. The convection column can tower to such great heights that it almost penetrates the outer boundary of the atmosphere. Within it, fire brands of pine cones and bits of bark and wood may be lifted 5,000 feet or more to fall to earth well in advance of the flame front. The spot fires that they ignite are pulled into the convection column by the in-draft winds. The energy of the column increases and the machine-like cycle continues. Thus the high-intensity fire releases enough energy to essentially create its own environment. It becomes an atmospheric force and relates more to a major thunderstorm than to an ordinary surface fire. The average rate of speed is not exceptionally great, as such fires move in surges. Forest destruction, although great, is not complete. There often remain unburned pockets of timber that are then able to begin the slow and quiet business of seeding in a new forest.

14.3 CAUSES OF WILDFIRES

According to the U.S. Forest Service, there are nine major causes of wildfires in the United States: lightning, campfires, smokers, debris burning, incendiary, equipment use, railroads, children, and miscellaneous.

Lightning is the cause of only one forest fire in ten in the United States. However, some regions are much more vulnerable to ignition by lightning than others. For example, between 1970 and 1973 the Pacific Coast states claimed that 32 percent of their wildfire starts were by lightning, while the Rocky Mountain states claimed 48 percent for the same period. Early detection and attack on lightning-set fires has been made possible by information received from radar tracking stations and weather satellites.

Smokers include anyone who uses tobacco in the form of cigarettes, cigars, or pipes. They start thousands of wildfires each year through ignorance or carelessness. Perhaps unconsciously they drop or throw lighted matches or cigarettes along roadways, in fields, or in the woods. Hunters, hikers, fishers, or even woods workers are at times careless. Wildfires caused by smokers were ranked first in the 1930s, but they hold third place now. Knowledge of this hazard that results from smoking may be one reason why most woods workers, especially in the West, now use snuff or chewing tobacco.

Debris burning is the cause of many fires in farm woodlands and suburban areas. These are started by landowners to eliminate trash or brush or to clear the land. Debris fires may get out of hand

and spread to nearby fields and woods. This category has moved from third to second place nationwide, and it is the largest cause of fires in the Lakes States. Most states require a burning permit for debris burning and have stringent rules pertaining to control of debris fires.

Incendiary fires are those set maliciously and willfully to burn the property of another person. This frequently is done to "get even" with someone or purposely to do harm. People who commit such acts are punishable by law and may be arrested, fined, and imprisoned. Incendiary fires have held the distinction of being the number one cause of wildfires most of the years since the 1940s.

Mechanical equipment, other than that of railroads, accounts for 2 to 5 percent of the wildfires in the United States. Equipment includes tractors, bulldozers, trucks, skidders, jeeps, chain saws, and any other type of equipment that employs gasoline or fuel oil.

Railroad operations are the cause of many wildfires. This category includes fires that spread out of control from prescribed burning of rights-of-way and discarded crossties. Years ago, during logging operations, coal- and wood-burning trains were employed to remove the logs from logging camps. These trains would spew hot ashes and sparks into the air, into the canopies of coniferous trees, and onto the ground, igniting the tinder and causing major forest fires. Today, with the use of diesel locomotives and changes in the mode of transport to trucking, forest fires started by logging operations have been reduced greatly. However, train operations still cause fires started by "hot boxes," overheated packing around wheel bearings.

Children-set wildfires, particularly those set by children less than 12 years old, account for about 6 to 9 percent of U.S. wildfires.

Miscellaneous wildfires, those that cannot be grouped within the previous categories, account for about 7 to 9 percent of each year's wildfires in the United States.

From the preceding analysis it can be seen that about 90 percent of the wildfires in this country are caused by people. Apparently, more emphasis could be put on cautions and preventive measures.

14.4 KINDS OF WILDFIRES

The cause of a fire usually determines what kind of burn results. Widlfires are listed in four categories, as follows:

Single-tree fires are those that burn in dry snags, possibly ignited by lightning or set on purpose to smoke out bees or game from den trees. Such burning snags are extremely dangerous in that sparks may be windblown from them and create surface fires where they fall.

Ground fires burn in humus (partly decayed organic matter) or thick peat layers. These burn slowly and smoulder rather than flame, and can burn for several months. The coastal plains of North and South Carolina and the boglands of the Lakes States are plagued with this problem. Because of root kill, ground fires are very destructive to all vegetation.

Surface fires burn on or near the ground in underbrush and leaf litter. These are the most common kind of fires; almost all forest fires begin as surface fires.

Crown fires burn in the tree crowns and usually occur only in the coniferous species because of their flammable foliage. Wind can make a crown fire spread very quickly through a forest.

14.5 PREVENTION AND CONTROL OF WILDFIRES

Prevention of wildfires and suppression of those that do get started are the objectives of fire-control planning. Since nine out of ten wildfires are caused by the activities or carelessness of people, attempts at prevention are worth making.

Fires caused by people have been reduced greatly by closing forests to hunters and campers during extremely dry seasons, stopping logging operations during hazardous periods, requiring permits for any type of burning operation, stringent enforcement of state laws against arson, and constantly using public safety advertisements with specific emphasis on caution about the use of fire in forests.

In prevention activities, the causes of fires are analyzed and a major plan is designed to provide prompt fire detection and prompt suppression. Detection of a fire in a forest in its early stages, before major destruction can take place, is a very significant part of fire management. Use of the fire tower (Figure 14-2) for spotting fires in their early stages has been of great value in this country.

Large maps are employed in reporting exact locations of fires to those who fight them. The maps are marked with circles centered upon the locations of fire towers or other points of observation. When a lookout spots smoke, he or she sights an *alidade* (Figure 14-3) at it and determines the *azimuth* bearing (the angular direction with respect to north), estimates the distance of the source of

Figure 14-2. Fire tower used for detection of fires. (Courtesy USDA Forest Service)

Figure 14-3. A lookout employing an alidade in locating position of a fire. (Courtesy USDA Forest Service)

smoke from the station, and notes any landmarks. This information is telephoned to the district ranger or central dispatcher, who obtains similar data from other lookouts. He or she then plots the azimuth bearings on a map. The location of the fire is indicated where the lines of sight from the various points of observation intersect. This process is called *triangulation*. The dispatcher is then able to send off suppression crews with information on the location and size of the fire, type of fuel, and how quickly the fire is spreading.

Many states in the Pacific Northwest and Canada have replaced many of their lookout towers by fire watch patrol planes. These planes, flying a precise and routine pattern, can cover vast areas and can give more specific details about fires that are located. However, coverage cannot be as continuous as it is from a tower, and in uniform terrain the ability of the pilot to be precise is less than that of the system of triangulation. Hence, where speed of reaction is most critical, in the Southeast and in California, planes are employed to supplement but not replace the towers.

While smoke is the first sign of a fire, observed smoke does not necessarily indicate a wildfire; it may be just a campfire or the burning of rubbish. Where lightning-caused fires are the principal problem, air patrols are most effective. When an existing fire has produced haze and smoke blankets through which ground patrols cannot see, air patrols are especially useful.

A new method for spotting a wildfire employs infrared detection. This has the ability to recognize the presence of a fire by the heat emitted by the fire, rather than from seeing its flames or smoke. This works well when the fire cannot be seen because of smoke. The infrared method also can measure the size of a fire and help determine its speed of spreading. It may also show the position of rivers, roads, and other landscape points through temperature differences and thus help show the best way to get to the fire area.

Another type of remote sensing is radar, which is especially useful in tracking lightning storms. The U.S. Weather Bureau employs radar to track cumulo-nimbus cloud formations, which are associated with thunderstorms. Pulses of microwave energy in narrow beams are reflected by a target such as a cloud formation.

From the time that a fire is first discovered to the time control actions can be applied, four events must happen: *discovery* of the fire; *report* of its presence and location; *getaway* of fire-fighting personnel; and *travel* to get to the fire. The time required for each of these steps needs to be made as brief as possible.

14.6 CONDITIONS THAT AFFECT SPREAD OF A WILDFIRE

A fire needs three things in order to burn—heat, fuel, and air. Without any one of these elements it cannot exist. In Section 14.2 the significant part played by wind was stressed, by providing an abundance of moving air. We have also discussed fuels on the forest floor in Section 14.1. Let us now look at the element of heat.

Most dry forest fuels must be heated to a temperature of 600 to 880°F (316 to 470°C) before they will ignite. When the moisture content of the fuel is high, more heat is needed because water must first be evaporated, and until it is gone, it tends to hold the material to the boiling-point temperature. A fire gains speed as it dries the fuel with its own heat. Green timber, which ordinarily will not ignite, is menaced by an accumulation of dry fuel in a nearby slash-covered area. The rate of spread of a fire is partially dependent upon the amount of fuel available to produce heat.

The direction and steepness of a slope and its surface condition also govern the spread rate and severity of a fire. Varied terrain and rugged country make the spread of a fire irregular, while topography that is level to rolling allows a fire to develop more uniformly. Steep slopes result in rapid and less predictable burning up slope. They favor more complete drying and heating of fuel ahead of the flame front. Southerly and westerly facing slopes burn more severely than those that face in the other direction because they are drier and warmer from direct exposure to the sun, but they generally tend to have less fuel.

14.7 SUPPRESSION OF WILDFIRES

Stopping a wildfire requires a change in the conditions conducive to its spread. There are two ways of suppressing a fire: direct and indirect. The direct attack consists of working on the burning edge of the fire. This method may be employed when the fire's rate of spread is low and the heat is not too great. The fire may be controlled by shoveling, raking, or sweeping burning material back into the fire. Beating out the flames by use of wet cloths or green branches can stop small fires. If water is available, it may be pumped onto a fire, as seen in Figure 14-4.

The indirect attack is to construct fire lanes such as are pictured

Figure 14-4. Water being used to suppress a fire set by children on private land. (Courtesy USDA Forest Service)

in Figures 14-5 through 14-7, and to rely upon natural barriers such as creeks or rivers to stop the spread. Such procedures are employed in fighting very hot, fast-spreading fires.

Backfires, when employed by experienced personnel, are a good way of suppressing a surface fire. As seen in Figure 14-8, backfires are set along natural barriers or plowed fire lines and are allowed to burn back to the wildfire. As the backing fire moves slowly into the wind and away from the firebreak, it creates an area in which there is no potential fuel for the advancing wildfire. This widens the firebreak and reduces the likelihood that burning embers will blow ahead of the fire and create a breakover or spot fires.

The North Carolina Division of Forest Resources and other organizations are using aerial ignition burns for backfiring, hazard reduction, and site preparation. An aerial ignition burn, illustrated in Figure 14-9, is fired by helicopter and also experimentally by airplane. Just prior to being dropped, plastic spheres similar to ping-pong balls that contain potassium permanganate ($KMnO_4$) are injected with a solution that consists of 50 percent water and 50 percent ethylene glycol (concentrated permanent antifreeze).

The reaction between the two chemicals produces, in a few seconds, an intense flame. This delay permits the ball to reach the forest floor, where the litter is ignited. The benefits of this technique

Figure 14-5. Mathis plow being used to create a firebreak down to mineral soil. (Courtesy USDA Forest Service)

Figure 14-6. Bulldozer making a fire lane near edge of a forest fire. (Courtesy USDA Forest Service)

Figure 14-7. Firebreak that has been constructed to prevent spread of a possible fire. (Courtesy USDA Forest Service)

Figure 14-8. Backfire being set after using a Mathis plow to cut a restraining fire ditch. (Courtesy USDA Forest Service)

Figure 14-9. Site preparation by aerial ignition employing ping-pong type balls loaded with $KMnO_4$ and ethylene glycol. (Courtesy North Carolina Division of Forest Resources)

are twofold: First, large areas can be ignited very quickly. This improves the safety of fire control and the economics of controlled burning. Second, when the balls are dropped in a very clear pattern, each small fire quickly burns into the areas of the adjacent fires so that no buildup of intensity is possible. With careful placement this technique is very safe. It is, however, a very new development, and most backfires and prescribed fires are still set by ground crews, as illustrated in Figure 14-8.

Another innovation in fire control is the use of fire retardants. These are chemicals that when applied to fuels alter the chemistry of combustion of these fuels. They may burn but do not flame. Thus the intensity of a fire advancing into an area coated with retardant is effectively starved and perhaps stopped. Because of this characteristic, retardants are most commonly employed to build or to reinforce existing fire lines in advance of a fire. They are little more effective than water when used directly on flaming fuels. The first retardant, sodium calcium borate, has largely been replaced by monammonium and diammonium phosphates and by ammonium sulfate, all of which are commercial fertilizers. These retardants can be delivered either by powerful pumps from tanker trucks or by aircraft (see Figure 14-10). The aircraft involved range from small agricultural planes to large military bomber or cargo planes modified

Figure 14-10. Borate slurry solution being pumped into bomb-bay tanks of a converted B-26 aircraft. (Courtesy USDA Forest Service)

to quickly dump from 600 to 2,000 gallons of retardant. The tactics of aerial delivery are complex and exacting, but the sight of a huge bomber spilling out thousands of gallons of retardant at a 300-foot altitude is exciting (see Figure 14-11).

14.8 FIRE SEASONS

A fire season has been defined by the U.S. Forest Service as the period or periods of the year during which frequency and severity of wildfire justify an organized and active system of control. In the northern, central, and southern forests there are two distinct fire seasons. One is in the spring, usually ending as new foliage emerges. The other is in the fall after foliage has fallen and cured. In general, the spring fire season lasts longer, but fires may be more intense in the fall. The long, hot, dry summers of the Rocky Mountains and the Pacific Northwest forest regions create a single fire season. All across the country, fires can occur whenever fuel volume,

Figure 14–11. Aerial suppression of a wildfire in Ozark National Forest in Arkansas. (Courtesy USDA Forest Service)

fuel moisture, and ignition source are suitable. During fire seasons one can expect this to happen more frequently and for the fires generally to burn more intensely.

14.9 SUMMARY

Fires in forests are part of the scheme of nature. There is evidence of vast fires in North America prior to our colonization. Whether a fire results in forest destruction or forest enhancement is a function of many environmental variables, such as weather, wind, topography, and fuel. The control or manipulation of the interaction between fire and these factors is known as fire management.

The causes of wildfires can be classified into nine major categories, of which the three most prevalent are lightning, incendiaries, and tobacco smokers. Less frequently, forest fires are started from debris burning, by campers, by children, and from the use of equipment. Since about nine out of ten forest fires are the result of human activities and carelessness, prevention is possible, and much progress has been made in that respect.

Modern methods of wildfire detection include the use of airplanes, helicopters, fire towers, good maps, visual sight, infrared detectors, and radar. Modern fire fighting in forests includes the use of Mathis plows (or flotation plows in coastal plains), bulldozers, and suppressant chemicals distributed by airplane. Backfires may be set by hand or by airplane.

The people involved in fire fighting usually are very capable and highly trained, and they place their lives on the line every time they are put into a fire situation. Unfortunately, most of the fires they face are caused by people, and millions of trees are destroyed because of stupidity or carelessness.

chapter 15

Forestry Service Assistance to Private Landowners

15.1 SOURCES OF FOREST MANAGEMENT ASSISTANCE

Today, by far most Americans live in urban or suburban areas on small bits of land, but some fortunate individuals find themselves living on land that includes wooded acres. For these people a number of forestry services are available, either provided by the government or purchasable by the owner with the aid of government advice or guidance.

Also, some commercial forestry firms offer forest management assistance. However, it is given with the stipulation that, should the landowner decide to sell the timber or land, the assisting firm will get first option to buy the property. The commercial forestry firm must, however, concur with the landowner's asking price or best offer for the land or timber. A letter of commitment to this effect is signed when the forest management assistance program is initiated.

The individual states have laws that provide for the service phases of forest assistance supplied by government sources to private landowners.

15.2 SERVICES SUPPLIED TO SMALL LANDOWNERS

Upon request, a state forester will accompany a landowner on a tour of the property and make a detailed examination of the forest land. The forester will discuss with the landowner objectives and priorities based on woodland needs. Then, based on the landowner's objectives and in harmony with the needs of the land, the forester prepares a plan of action for the property in the form of a forest management plan.

Regardless of whether the landowner wants to manage forest land for income timber, for enjoyment of wildlife, clean water, recreation, or any combination of these benefits, foresters can provide the expertise necessary to implement the plan. In many states the forest management plan must be in writing and be approved by the secretary of natural resources and community development or his or her representative. The plan is then presented to the landowner with recommendations, stating which of the many forest practices he or she should consider for the woodland.

Figures 15-1 through 15-3 show an example of such a management plan prepared by the service forester of Durham County, North Carolina, to assist the owner of 20 acres of woods that had been, in Civil War days, part of a cotton farm. Note that the forester chose to consider and evaluate the 20 acres in four areas and to supply different suggestions as to what might be done with each. Such a management plan serves to achieve the landowner's immediate objectives while providing adequate environmental protection and ensuring maximum productive value to future generations. A landowner is free of course to make his or her own plan, but many prefer to have this done by a professional forester.

The state of North Carolina and most other states provide a variety of assistance to private woodland owners. These include engineering design for dams for fish ponds, fish stocking, production and sale at cost of forest tree seedlings, fire detection and control, advice and assistance on forest disease and insect control, timber marking for stand improvement, and practices to promote reforestation.

15.3 COST-SHARING PROGRAMS

A major part of privately owned forest land in the United States is held by people who do not have the money for long-term investments. This is one of the primary reasons for the establishment of

DIVISION OF
FOREST RESOURCES

Ralph C. Winkworth, Director

Box 27687, Raleigh 27611
Telephone 919 733-2162

North Carolina Department of Natural Resources & Community Development

James B. Hunt, Jr., Governor   Howard N. Lee, Secretary

Division of Forest Resources
Route # 3, Box 186-1A
Hillsborough, N. C. 27278
June 4, 1979

D-11 - FM
Project - Durham County
Githens, Sherwood

Mr. Sherwood Githens
4427 Chapel Hill Road
Durham, North Carolina 27707

Dear Mr. and Mrs. Githens:

The recent two visits with you were quite enjoyable. I am enclosing a brief summary of our discussion and recommendations on the woodland area of your homestead.

You will note that I am suggesting a possible complete harvest cut on the main portion of your older pine areas, leaving a rim or border of some 100-150 feet uncut as a screen and frame for your home and extensive lawn down to the highway. It is proposed that we would outline this cutting boundary with paint, and the timber be estimated and sold probably by a consulting forester. The market for this type of timber is quite strong now.

On the other hand, you would, of course, be subjected to considerable noise with chain saws and tree length skidders roaring in the woods. Also, the log trucks would need access to the highway either down your driveway or more likely just to the west of your yard. Then, too, the recommended follow-up site preparation several months later would involve some bulldozer work with attendant noise. You are already more or less involved with a planned road change and widening project, so this might be entirely too much commotion for one year. In such case you may well decide to hold your woodland as is for at least five years, realizing that some loss of growth may be justified under the circumstances.

(concluded on next page)

Figure 15-1. Example of a woodland management plan prepared by a North Carolina service forester. (Courtesy North Carolina Department of Natural Resources)

I will say that we would be happy to work with you and the contractors if you decide upon a harvest cut and reforestation project. I think with the Forestry Incentives Program cost-sharing you could figure on a net cost to you of about $50-$60 per acre for such reforestation. Naturally the area, although somewhat screened, would not look very attractive until the young pines get 4-6 feet high. This would be about four (4) years hence.

In any event, we will be glad to mark the two small patches of younger pine on either side of your yard for a first pulpwood thinning. The usual short wood pulpwood truck leaves little permanent evidence of a woods road, and generally the thinned areas have a much better appearance in a brief period of time. I may say that we have quite recently marked a few cords of pulpwood for such a thinning on Dr. John Couch's property just across the creek. Possibly one operator could arrange to do the cutting on both tracts.

I will be glad to answer any other questions you may have about this plan or other forestry matters.

Very truly yours,

Virgil G. Watkins,
Service Forester

VGW/ek

cc: Bill Colville, County Ranger

Figure 15-1. (*continued*)

cost-sharing programs designed to enhance and protect the forest resources of the United States. These programs were developed to share the improvement expense of the private forest landowner who is eligible for such assistance.

It must be emphasized that these programs are not permanent and are subject to changes or even to liquidation, much like the "soil bank" program that was very popular in the United States at one time, but no longer exists. We will here discuss three governmental funding programs now in progress. They are the Forest Development Program (FDP), the Forestry Incentives Program (FIP), and the Agriculture Conservation Program (ACP). The first of these is an example of a state program; the other two are federal.

The *Forest Development Program* is a North Carolina program that is intended to encourage private landowners to reforest after a timber harvest and to put their idle and underproductive land into full timber production. Applications are accepted from any individual, group, association, or corporation. To qualify, the applicant must own land that is suitable for growing commercial timber. The amount of land the applicant owns has no bearing upon eligibility.

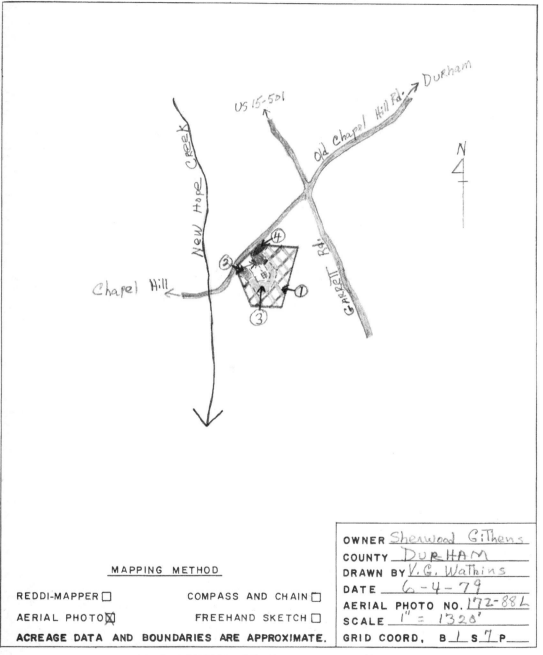

Figure 15-2. Map of small woodland property drawn by forester. (Courtesy North Carolina Department of Natural Resources)

N. C. DIVISION OF FOREST RESOURCES

Department of Natural Resources and Community Development

WOODLAND MANAGEMENT PLAN

NAME: Mr. Sherwood Githens   DATE: 6-4-79

ADDRESS: 4427 Chapel Hill Road, Durham, N. C. 27707

*Area or Field Number	Approx. No of Acres		Forest Type or Species and Approx. Age	Recommended Management Practices and Prescription For Carrying Out Treatment	When Practice Should Be Done, By Whom and Other Information
	Woods	Other			
1	12		Loblolly and short-leaf pine - Natural stands mostly 55-60 years old. Selectively logged about 20 years ago.	Consider final harvest cut 1979-80, to be followed with site preparation and planting to loblolly pine seedlings about 1 year later. Hold natural border of thinned and uncut timber around home site and highway (2,3,4)- Alternative plan would be to hold all timber as is for 5 yrs.	Should be eligible for cost-sharing under Forestry Incentives Program at about 60 percent of total cost of reforestation.
2	3		Loblolly pine on former open land 18-22 years old.	Make first thinning for pulpwood in 1979 to maintain good growth rate and improve appearance.	Marking by N. C. Forest Service at regular charge of 20 cents per cord. Cutting by regular crew producing pine pulpwood.
3	4		Border Strip of older pine stand as in Area #1 to be retained for scenic beauty.	N. C. Forest Service will outline and mark cutting border with paint upon request.	
4	1		Mixed hardwood area bordering highway and yard.	May have light improvement cut to enhance aesthetic value of homestead.	

* "Area or Field No." above corresponds to same number shown on <u>WOODLAND MANAGEMENT MAP</u>

PREPARED BY: *V. G. Watkins*
V. G. Watkins,
Service Forester

PREVENT FOREST FIRES !   **GROW MORE TIMBER CROPS!**

Figure 15-3.   Woodland management plan for the estate of Dr. Sherwood Githens, Jr. (Courtesy North Carolina Department of Natural Resources)

If an applicant is eligible, any work needed to establish a new forest may be conducted according to an approved plan. Such work may include the work needed for site preparation and tree planting, including the cost of the seedlings. Also included are use of methods for releasing the seedling and sprouts of valuable species from competing vegetation. These practices apply to management of hardwoods as well as to pines.

As to the extent of financial assistance available, the landowner may be reimbursed 60 percent of the actual per acre cost, or 60 percent of the prevailing rate in that region, whichever is less. The landowner may receive assistance on a maximum of 100 acres per year. Prevailing regional rates for typical forestry practices are set by the secretary of natural resources and community development.

A question often asked is, "Can you receive both state and federal cost-sharing funds?" The answer is yes, but not on the same acreage. The North Carolina Forest Development Program is designed to supplement the Federal Forest Incentive program, not to duplicate it. Funding for all these programs may be arranged through the local county Agriculture Stabilization Conservation Service (ASCS). The state forestry agency must certify that the project has been completed satisfactorily so that the owner's cost-sharing payments can be made by the county ASCS office.

The *Forestry Incentives Program* was authorized by Congress in 1973 to share the cost of forestry practices that vary slightly from those mentioned for the state FDP program. However, the federal share of the costs ranges up to 75 percent, depending on the cost-share rate set in the particular state and county by the Agricultural Stabilization and Conservation (ASC) Committee. To be eligible for this program, the landowner must:

1. Own a tract of no more than 1,000 acres of eligible forest land.
2. Be a private landowner (individual, group, association, or corporation not primarily engaged in manufacturing forest products or providing public utility services).
3. Have land suitable for reforestation or for improved management.
4. Have land capable of producing marketable timber crops meeting minimum productivity standards; at least 10 acres.

Whether or not a potential applicant's county is participating in the FIP program may be determined by inquiring at the local ASCS office, an Extension Service office, or of the local state forester.

These offices are able to explain the FIP and other programs in much more detail than space permits in this text.

The *Agriculture Conservation Program* is a federally funded, cost-sharing program with services and practices that nearly parallel those already discussed. However, this applies to landowners with much smaller acreage, such as 2-, 3-, or 5-acre plots.

15.4 SUMMARY

Most of the forestry activities described in this book are carried out in a large-scale setting, in the interests of the public in general, or of the government, or of commercial organizations that produce and sell wood products. However, there is also a division of forestry concerned with serving the owners of small farms and wooded homesteads. Such people can obtain technical advice at no charge by requesting it from the nearest service forester, through the county agricultural office. The forester can arrange to tour the woodland or farm with the owner, after which he or she will prepare and supply a written woodland management plan designed to maximize utilization of the land as a renewable resource. The county agent also is in a position to make the owner aware of several sources of state or federal money for which the landowner may be eligible to assist in paying for reforestation or stand improvement.

Bibliography

PRIMARY REFERENCE SOURCES

Books

Allen, Shirley, W., and Leonard, Justin W. *Conserving Natural Resources,* 3rd ed. New York: McGraw-Hill, 1966.

Avery, Eugene T. *Forest Measurements.* New York: McGraw-Hill, 1967.

——. *Natural Resources Measurements,* 2nd ed. New York: McGraw-Hill, 1975.

Barney, Daniel. *The Last Stand: Ralph Nader's Study Group Report on the National Forests.* New York: Grossman, 1974.

Barrett, John W. *Regional Silviculture of the United States,* Rev. ed. New York: Ronald Press, 1962.

Baxter, Dow V. *Pathology in Forest Practice.* New York: John Wiley, 1952.

Behn, Harry, compiler. *Cricket Songs: Japanese Haiku.* New York: Harcourt Brace Jovanovich, 1964.

Bendick, Jeanne. *Adaptation.* New York: Franklin Watts, 1971.

Bowen, Catherine Drinker. *The Most Dangerous Man in America; Scenes from the Life of Benjamin Franklin.* Boston-Toronto: Little, Brown, 1974.

Boyce, John Shaw. *Forest Pathology,* 3rd ed. New York: McGraw-Hill, 1961.

Brandon, William. *The Magic World: American Indian Songs and Poems.* New York: Morrow, 1972.

Brockman, Frank C., Zim, Herbert S., and Merri, Lees. *Trees of North America.* New York: Western Publishing Co., 1968.

Brown, Arthur A., and Davis, Kenneth P. *Forest Fire: Control and Use*, 2nd ed. New York: McGraw-Hill, 1973.

Brown, D.G. *Exploring and Understanding Plant Structure.* Westchester, Ill.; Benefic Press, 1974.

Brown, Leslie. *Africa: A Natural History.* New York: Random House, 1965.

Brown, Nelson C., and Bethel, James S. *Lumber*, 2nd ed. New York: John Wiley, 1958.

Busch, Phyllis S. *At Home in Its Habitat: Animal Neighborhoods.* Cleveland, Ohio: Collins-World, 1970.

Butler, D.M. *American Conservation.* Washington, D.C.: American Forestry Association, 1935.

Cailliet, Greg, and others. *Everyman's Guide to Ecological Living.* New York: Macmillan, 1971.

Carron, L.T. *An Outline of Forest Mensuration.* Canberra, Australia: Australian National University Press, 1968.

Chapman, Herman H., and Meyer, Walter H. *Forest Mensuration.* New York: McGraw-Hill, 1949.

——. *Forest Valuation.* New York: McGraw-Hill, 1947.

Chase, Stuart. *Some Things Worth Knowing.* New York: Harper & Row, 1958.

Clark, J.D. *Kalambo Falls Prehistoric Site.* Vol. 1. *The Geology, Paleoecology, and Detailed Stratigraphy of the Excavations.* New York: Cambridge University Press, 1969. Reviewed in *Science*, 169 (1970), pp. 44–45.

Collins, Stephen. *Forest and Woodland.* The Community of Living Things Series. Mankato, Minn.: Creative Educational Society, 1967.

Cormack, Maribelle. *The First Book of Trees.* New York: Franklin Watts, 1951.

Coulson, Robert N., and others. *The Southern Pine Beetle.* Publication 108. College Station, Tex.: Texas Forest Service, 1961–1971.

Daniel, T.W., Helms, J.A., and Baker, F.S. *Principles of Siviculture.* 2nd ed. New York: McGraw-Hill, 1979.

Dasmann, R.F. *Environment Conservation*, 2nd ed. New York: John Wiley, 1968.

Davis, Kenneth P. *Forest Fire: Control and Use.* New York: McGraw-Hill, 1959.

DeBell, Garrett, ed. *The Environmental Handbook: Prepared for the First National Environmental Teach-In.* New York: Ballantine, 1970.

Dudley, Ruth N. *Our American Trees.* New York: Thomas Y. Crowell, 1956.

Eadie, W. Robert. *Animal Control in Field, Farm and Forest.* New York: Macmillan, 1954.

Ehrenfeld, David W. *Biological Conservation.* New York: Holt, Rinehart and Winston, 1970.

Farb, Peter. *The Forest.* Morristown, N.J.: Silver Burdett, 1969.

Fenton, Carroll L., and Pallas, Dorothy C. *Trees and Their World.* New York: John Day, 1957.

Fernow, B.E. *History of Forestry.* Toronto, Canada: n.p., 1911.

Frank, Bernard, and Netboy, Anthony. *Water, Land and People.* New York: Knopf, 1950.

Graham, Kenneth. *Concepts of Forest Entomology.* New York: Van Nostrand Reinhold, 1963.

Graham, Samuel A., and Knight, Fred B. *Principles of Forest Entomology.* New York: McGraw-Hill, 1965.

Harlow, William M., Harrar, Ellwood S., and White, Fred M. *Textbook of Dendrology.* New York: McGraw-Hill, 1979.

Hawes, Judy. *What I Like about Toads.* New York: Thomas Y. Crowell, 1972.

Helfman, Elizabeth S. *Land, People and History.* New York: D. McKay, 1962.

——. *Maypoles and Wood Demons: The Meaning of Trees.* New York: Seabury, 1972.

Hirsch, S. Carl. *Guardians of Tomorrow: Pioneers in Ecology.* New York: Viking, 1971.

Hopke, William E., editor-in-chief. *The Encyclopedia of Careers and Vocational Guidance, Careers and Occupations*, 3rd ed. Chicago: J.G. Ferguson, 1975.

Hurd, Edith T. *This Is the Forest.* New York: Coward-McCann, 1969.

Husch, Bertram, Miller, Charles I., and Beers, T.W. *Forest Mensuration*, 2nd ed. New York: Ronald Press, 1972.

Illick, Joseph S. *An Outline of General Forestry.* New York: Barnes and Noble, 1935.

——. *An Outline of General Forestry.* 3rd ed. New York: Barnes & Noble, 1939.

Kane, Henry B. *Four Seasons in the Woods.* New York: Knopf, 1968.

Keen, Martin L. *The World Beneath Our Feet: The Story of Soil.* New York: Messner, 1974.

Kittredge, Joseph. *Forest Influences.* McGraw-Hill, 1948.

Kozlowski, T.T. *Growth and Development of Trees*, Vol. II: *Cambial Growth, Root Growth, and Reproductive Growth.* New York: Academic Press, 1971.

Kramer, Paul J., and Kozlowski, T. *Physiology of Trees.* New York: McGraw-Hill, 1960.

Laycock, George. *Animal Movers: A Collection of Ecological Surprises.* Garden City, N.Y.: Doubleday, 1971.

Lull, Howard W. *Handbook of Applied Hydrology*, edited by Ven Te Chow. Section 6: *Ecological and Silvicultural Aspects.* New York: McGraw-Hill, 1964.

McClung, Robert M. *Lost Wild America.* New York: Morrow, 1969.

McCormick, Jack. *The Life of the Forest.* New York: McGraw-Hill, 1966.

McCulloch, Walter F. *Woods Words: A Comprehensive Dictonary of Loggers' Terms.* Portland, Ore: Historical Society, 1958.

McLuhan, T.C. *Touch the Earth: A Self Portrait of Indian Existence.* New York: Dutton, 1971.

Mumford, Lewis. *Technics and Civilizations.* New York: Harcourt Brace Jovanovich, 1934.

Nash, Roderick, ed. *The American Environment: Reading in the History of Conservation.* Reading, Mass.: Addison-Wesley, 1968.

Nash, Roderick. *The American Conservation Movement.* Saint Charles, Ill.: Forum, 1974.

Nicklesburg, Janet. *Ecology: Habitats, Niches and Food Chains.* Philadelphia: Lippincott, 1969.

Odum, Eugene P. *Ecology.* New York: Holt, Rinehart and Winston, 1975.

Pack, Charles L., and Gill, Tom. *Forest and Mankind*. New York: Macmillan, 1930.

Pearce, J. Kenneth, and Stenzel, George. *Logging and Pulpwood Production*. New York: Ronald Press, 1972.

Peet, Bill. *Farewell to Shady Glade*. Boston: Houghton Mifflin, 1966.

Peterson, Bonnie, ed. *Dawn of the World: Coast Miwok Myths*. Woodacre, Calif.: Impressions, 1976. (Published in cooperation with the Marin Museum Society)

Petrides, George A. *A Field Guide to Trees and Shrubs*, 2nd ed. Boston: Houghton Mifflin, 1973.

Preston, R.J. *North American Trees*. Ames, Iowa: Iowa State College Press, 1950.

Pringle, Laurence. *Into the Woods: Exploring the Forest Ecosystem*. New York: Macmillan, 1973.

———. *Chains, Webs, and Pyramids: The Flow of Energy in Nature*. New York: Crowell, 1975.

Reid, Keith. *Nature's Network*. Garden City: N.Y.: Doubleday, 1970.

Rich, Louise D. *The First Book of Lumbering*. New York: Franklin Watts, 1967.

Ricklefs, Robert E. *Ecology*. Portland, Ore.: Chiron Press, 1973.

Rue, Leonard L. *World of the White Tailed Deer*. Philadelphia: Lippincott, 1962.

Satterlund, Donald R. *Watershed Management*. New York: Ronald Press, 1972.

Schwartz, George I. *Life in a Log*. Garden City, N.Y.: Doubleday, 1972.

Seton, Ernest Thompson. *Lives of Game Animals*, Vol. 3. *Hoofed Animals*. New York: Literary Guild of America, 1909.

Sharpe, Grant W., Hendee, Clare W., and Allen, Shirley W. *Introduction to Forestry*, 4th ed. New York: McGraw-Hill, 1976.

Shirley, Hardy L. *Forestry and Its Career Opportunities*, 3rd ed. New York: McGraw-Hill, 1973.

Smith, Agnes. *An Edge of the Forest*, 2nd ed. Parsons, W.Va.: McClain, 1974.

Smith, David M. *The Practice of Silviculture*, 7th ed. New York: John Wiley, 1962.

Smith, Frances D. *The First Book of Conservation*. New York: Franklin Watts, 1972.

Society of American Foresters. *Terminology of Forest Science, Technology, Practice and Products*. Cambridge, England: W. Heffer and Sons, 1971; (English Language Edition) Washington, D.C.: Ford-Robertson, 1971; (Multilingual) Washington, D.C.: n.p., 1971.

Spurr, S.H. *Forest Inventory*. New York: Ronald Press, 1952.

Storer, John H. *The Web of Life*. New York: New American Library, 1972.

Towmey, James W., and Horstian, Clarence F. *Foundations of Silviculture upon an Ecological Basis*, 2nd ed. (revised by C.F. Koristian). New York: John Wiley, 1947.

Van den Bosch, Robert, and Messenger, P.S. *Biological Control*. New York: Intext Educational Publishers, 1973.

Wackerman, A.E., Hagenstein, W.D., and Mitchell, A.S. *Harvesting Timber Crops*, 2nd ed. New York: McGraw-Hill, 1966.

Winters, Robert K. *The Forest and Man*. New York: Vantage Press, 1974.

Zim, Herbert S. *Trees: A Guide to Familiar American Trees*. Golden Book Series. Racine, Wisc.: Western Publishing Company, 1952.

Periodicals

Abbott, H.G., and Eliason, E.J. "Forestry Tree Nursery Practices in the United States." *Journal of Forestry* 66 (1968): 704-11.

Allen, E.T. "50,000 Firebrands." *American Forests* 45 (1939): 178-79, 239.

Baker, Frederick S. "A Revised Tolerance Table." *Journal of Forestry* 47 (1949): 179-81.

Baker, Whiteford L. "Forest Insect and Research Control." *Journal of Forestry* 57 (1959): 243-44.

Barrows, Jack S. "Forest Fire Research for Environment Protection." *Journal of Forestry* 69 (1971): 17-20.

Benedict, W.V. "Every Forester Has a Stake in Forest Insect Spraying." *Journal of Forestry* 57(1959): 245-49.

Bennett, H.H. "Fire, Floods, and Erosion." *American Forests* 45 (1939): 174-77, 229.

Borgeson, Lillian. "Wild Colors, Natural Dyes." *National Wildlife* 15 (April-May 1977): 50.

Brender, E.V., and Cooper, R.W. "Prescribed Burning in Georgia's Piedmont Loblolly Pine Stands." *Journal of Forestry* 66 (1968): 31-36.

Brickell, James E. "More on Diameter Tape and Calipers." *Journal of Forestry* 68 (1970).

Bruce, Mason B. "National Forest in Alaska." *Journal of Forestry* 58 (1960): 437-442.

Cadzow, Donald A. "Ancient Dwellers of the Ozarks" *American Forests and Forest Life* 31 (1924): 70.

Cammerer, Arno B. "Outdoor Recreation—Gone with the Flames." *American Forests* 45 (1939): 182-85.

Chapman, H.H. "Effect of Fire in Preparation of Seedbed for Longleaf Pine Seedlings." *Journal of Forestry* 34 (1936): 852-854.

Craig, James B. "Herding Fires." *American Forests* 39 (1975): 50-51.

Croker, T.C., Jr. "Crop Seedling Method for Planning Brown Spot Burns in Longleaf Pine." *Journal of Forestry* 65 (1967): 488.

Curtis, Robert O., and Rushmore, F.M. "Some Effects of Stand Density and Deer Browsing on Reproduction in an Adirondack Forest Stand." *Journal of Forestry* 56 (1958): 116-121.

Dana, Samuel T. "Fire over the Lake States." *American Forests* 45 (1939): 170-72.

Dane, C.W. "The Hidden Environmental Cost of Alternative Materials Available for Construction." *Journal of Forestry* 70 (1972): 734-736.

Diller, Jesse D., and Clapper, Russell B. "A Progress Report on Attempts to Bring Back the Chestnut Tree in the Eastern United States." *Journal of Forestry* 63 (1954-1964): 186-188.

Dowden, P.B. "What about Biological Control?" *Journal of Forestry* 57 (1959): 267-270.

Doxey, Wall. "Fire or Forestry—The South's Great Problem." *American Forests* 39 (1939): 161-64.

Gabrileson, Ira N. "Burning Wildlife." *American Forests* 45 (1939): 186-87.

Gara, Robert I. "What We Have Learned from New Research on the Southern Pine Beetle." *Forest Farmer* 25 (1966): 6-7, 18-19.

"Great Fires of the Past." *American Forests* 45 (1939): 160.

Greeley, William B. "The Red Paradox of Conservation." *American Forests* 45 (1939): 153–57.

Haig, I.T. "Fire in Modern Management." *Journal of Forestry* 36 (1938): 1045–49.

Hepting, George H. "How Forest Disease and Insect Research Is Paying Off. The Case for Forest Pathology." *Journal of Forestry* 68 (1970): 78–81.

Hirst, Eric. "Living Off the Fuels of the Land." *Natural History* 82 (December 1973): 20–22.

Holbrook, Stewart N. "When Peshtigo Burned." *American Forests* 45 (1939): 158–60.

Hook, D.D., and Stubbs, Jack, "Selection Cutting and Reproduction of Cherrybark and Shumark Oaks." *Journal of Forestry* 63 (1965): 927–29.

Jacobs, Rodney D. "Growth and Development of Deer-browsed Sugar Maple Seedlings." *Journal of Forestry* 67 (1965): 870–74.

Jayaweera, K.O.L.F., and Ahlanas, Kristina. "Detection of Thunderstorms from Satellite Imagery for Forest Fire Control." *Journal of Forestry* 72 (1974): 767–70.

Johnston, Patricia. "Benjamin Franklin and Fire Insurance." *Early American Life* IX (1978): 30–33.

Judd, C.S. "Forestry in Hawaii." *Journal of Forestry* 33 (1935): 1005–6.

Kelts, Lora I. "International Directory of Professional Forestry Associations and Their Principal Publications." *Journal of Forestry* 8 (1973): 506–11.

Kozlowski, T.T. "Light and Water Relations to Growth and Competition of Piedmont Forest Tree Species." *Ecology Monogram* 19 (1949): 207–231.

Kramer, P.J., Oosting, J.J., and Korstian, C.F. "Survival of Pine and Hardwood Seedlings in Forest and Open." *Ecology* 33 (1952): 427–30.

Leaky, Melvin M. "Finding the World's Earliest Man." *National Geographic* (1966): 420–438.

Line, Les, and Perry, J.D. "Snowmobiles: Love'em or Hate'em." *National Wildlife* 10 (1971): 21–22.

Long, John E. "The Menace of Stills." *American Forests* 62 (1956): 36–39.

Lutz, H.J. "Forest Ecosystems: Their Maintenance, Amelioration, and Deterioration." *Journal of Forestry* 61 (August 1963): 563–569.

Lysons, Hilton N., and Twito, Roger H. "Skyline Logging: An Economical Means of Reducing Environmental Impact of Logging." *Journal of Forestry* 71 (1973): 580–83.

Makhikjani, A.B., and Lichtenberg, A.J. "Energy and Well-Being." *Environment* 14 (June 1972): 10–18.

McDonald, Phillip M., and Whiteley, Raymond V. "Logging a Roadside Stand to Protect Scenic Values." *Journal of Forestry* 70 (1972) 80–83.

Meyer, N. Arthur. "Conquerors—Forest Destroyers of the Andes." *American Forests* 51 (1945): 178–79, 200.

Nickerson, Roy. "Forests Are Personal." *American Forests* 78 (September 1972): 32–35.

Oosting, H.J. "An Ecological Analysis of the Plant Communities of Piedmont, North Carolina." *American Midland Naturalist.* 28 (1942): 1–126.

Payne, Melvin M. "Preserving the Treasures of Olduvai Gorge." *National Geographic* 130 (1966): 701–09.

Peters, Penn A. "Balloon Logging: A Look at Current Operating System." *Journal of Forestry* 71 (1973): 577–79.

Reynolds, R.V., and Pierson, A.H. "Tracking the Sawmill Westward." *American Forests and Forest Life* 31 (1925): 646.

Smith, R.A., and Smith, C.M. "Aesthetics and Environmental Education." *Journal of Aesthetic Education* 4 (1970): 125–140.

Sumwalt, Eugene V. "The Alaska Public Domain." *Journal of Forestry* 58 (1960): 443–47.

"The South Moves against Wildfire." *American Forests* 62 (1956): 14–35.

Thomte, Walter L. "Mining the Taconite—The Story of Eries Mining Company." *Mining Engineering* (May 1963).

Tierson, William C., Patric, Earl F., and Brehrend, Donald F. "Influence of White Tailed Deer on the Logged Northern Hardwood Forest." *Journal of Forestry* 64 (1966): 801–05.

"Timber Demand Forecast for 1975." *Japan Lumber Journal* (May 31, 1969): 1, 4.

Vetz, George, and Johnson, Donald L. "Breaking the Web." *Environment* 16 (December 1974): 31–39.

Vogel, Richard J. "Monotonous Monocultures." *Ecology Today*, 1 (September 1971): 43.

Wahlenberg, W.G. "Forest Succession in the Southern Piedmont Region." *Journal of Forestry* 47 (1949): 713–15.

Waring, R.H., and Major, J. "Some Vegetation of the California Coastal Redwood Region in Relation to Gradients of Moisture, Nutrients, Light and Temperature." *Ecology Monogram* 32 (1964): 167–215.

"What Forests Mean to America." [Two page spread of art and words.] *American Forests* 82 (1976).

Winters, Robert K. "How Forestry Became a Part of FAO." *Journal of Forestry* 69 (1971): 574–78, 711.

Zuzanek, Jiri. "Society of Leisure or the Harried Leisure Class?" Leisure Trends in Industrial Societies. *Journal of Leisure Research* 6 (1974): 293–304.

Federal and State Government Publications

North Carolina Department of Natural Resources and Community Development. Division of Forest Resources. "Fire Terminology." Chap. 5, *Basic Fire Control Training Manual.* 1979.

United Nations. Food and Agriculture Organization Secretariat. "Wood Trends and Prospects," *Unasylva*, Vol. 20. Rome, Italy: United Nations Publication, 1966.

U.S. Department of Agriculture. "Forest Fire Management: For Ecology and People," by Jack S. Barrows in *Fire Management*, vol. 39, no. 3, 1973.

———. "Oak Wilt, A New Threat," by T.W. Bretz in *Plant Diseases.* Yearbook of Agriculture. Washington, D.C.: USDA, 1953.

———. "Littleleaf in Pines in the Southeast," by W.A. Campbell, O.L. Copeland, and G.H. Hepting in *Plant Diseases.* Yearbook of Agriculture. Washington, D.C.: USDA, 1953.

———. "Insects in the Forest: A Survey," by F.C. Craighead and John Miller in *Trees.* Yearbook of Agriculture. Washington, D.C.: USDA, 1949.

——. Forest Pest Management Group. *Insects and Disease of the Trees in the South.* Atlanta: USDA, 1972.

——. Agricultural Stabilization and Conservation Service. *Forestry Incentives Program for the Forest Landowner* (Cost Share Help).

——. *Shelter Belts for the Northern Great Plains,* by E.J. George. Farmer's Bulletin No. 2109. Washington, D.C.: USDA, 1961.

——. "Dwarf Mistletoes," by Lake S. Gill and Jess L. Bedwell in *Trees.* Yearbook of Agriculture. Washington, D.C.: USDA, 1949.

——. "Induced Tree Diseases and Insects." by G.F. Gravatt and D.E. Parker in *Trees.* Yearbook of Agriculture. Washington, D.C.: USDA, 1949.

——. "Fire as a Tool in Southern Pine," by A.W. Hartman in *Trees.* Yearbook of Agriculture, Washington, D.C.: USDA, 1949.

——. "Machines and Fires in the South," by A.W. Hartman in *Trees.* Yearbook of Agriculture. Washington, D.C.: USDA, 1949.

——. "Heart Rot," by George H. Hepting and James W. Kimmey in *Trees.* Yearbook of Agriculture. Washington, D.C.: USDA, 1949.

——. "Disease and the Forest," by L.M. Hutchins in *Trees.* Yearbook of Agriculture. Washington, D.C.: USDA, 1949.

——. "Bark Beetles," by F.P. Keene in *Trees.* Yearbook of Agriculture. Washington, D.C.: USDA, 1949.

——. *Forest Trees and Forest Regions of the United States,* by Wilbur R. Mattoon. Miscellaneous Publication No. 217. Washington, D.C.: USDA, 1936.

——. "The Effects of Soil Fertility," by G.L. McNew in *Plant Diseases.* Yearbook of Agriculture. Washington, D.C.: USDA, 1953.

——. "The Key to Protection," by S.A. Rohwer in *Trees.* Yearbook of Agriculture. Washington, D.C.: USDA, 1949.

——. "Dutch Elm Disease," by R.V. Swingle, R.R. Whitten, and E.G. Brewer in *Trees.* Yearbook of Agriculture. Washington, D.C.: USDA, 1949.

——. *The Nation's Renewable Resources, An Assessment, 1975.* Forest Resource Report No. 21. Washington, D.C.: USDA, 1977.

U.S. Department of Agriculture. Forest Service. *Eastern Forest Insects,* by Whiteford L. Baker. Miscellaneous Publication No. 1175. 1972.

——. "Shelter-Wood-Strip Harvesting Pattern with Full-Tree Skidding to Regenerate Red Pine," by R.W. Benzie and Z.A. Zasada. Note NC-132. Washington, D.C.: USDA, 1972.

——. "Development of Longleaf Pine Seedlings under Parent Trees," by W.D. Boyer, Research Paper SO-4. Washington, D.C.: USDA, 1963.

——. "Stump Sprouting after Harvest Cutting in Swamp Tupelo," by Dean S. DeBell. Res. Pap. SE-83. Washington, D.C.: USDA, 1971.

——. Division of Forest Pest Control. *Forest Insect and Disease Conditions in the United States.* Washington, D.C.: USDA, 1972.

——. *Great Forest Fires of America.* Washington, D.C.: USDA, 1936.

——. *A Forest Atlas of the South.* Southern Forest Experiment Station, New Orleans and Southeastern Forest Experiment Station, Asheville, N.C., 1969.

——. "Hunters and Hunting: Management Implications of Research," in Proceedings Recreation Applications Workshop. Asheville, N.C.: USDA, 1975.

——. *Biology and Classification of Dwarf Mistletoe* (arceuthobium), by Frank G. Hawksworth and Delbert Wiens. Handbook No. 401. Washington, D.C.: USDA, 1972.

——. "Early Development of Sweetgum Root Sprouts in Coastal South Carolina," by D.D. Hook, and others. Res. Pap. SE-62. Washington, D.C.: USDA, 1970.

——. "Deer Browsing in Northern Hardwoods after Clearcutting," by James S. Jordan. Res. Pap. NE-57. Washington, D.C.: USDA, 1967.

——. *The Timber Resource Situation in the United States*, by H.R. Josephson and Dwight Hair. Washington, D.C.: USDA, 1970.

——. *The Economic Importance of Timber in the United States*, by Dwight Hair. Misc. Pub. 941. Washington, D.C.: USDA, 1963.

——. "Managing the Family Forest," by Gordon G. Mark and Robert S. Dimmick. *Farmer's Bulletin*, vol. 2187. Washington, D.C.: USDA, 1963.

——. "Impacts of an Intensified Timber Management Program," by William McKillop. Res. Pap. WO-23. Washington, D.C: USDA, 1974.

——. "Methodology Used for 1975 Outdoor Recreation Projections." USDA (unpublished).

——. *National Forest Log Scaling Handbook*. Washington, D.C.: USDA, 1969.

——. "Timber Growing and Logging Practice in the Southwest and in the Black Hills Region," by G.A. Pearson and R.E. Marsh. Tech. Bull. No. 480. Washington, D.C.: USDA, 1935.

——. "Use of Openings in Spruce-Fir Forests of Arizona by Elk, Deer, and Cattle," by H.G. Reynolds. Note TM-66. Washington, D.C.: USDA, 1966.

——. *Silvics of Forest Trees of the United States*. Department of Agriculture Handbook. No. 271. Washington, D.C.: USDA, 1965.

——. *Silvicultural Systems for the Major Forest Types of the United States*. Department of Agriculture Handbook. No. 445. Washington, D.C.: USDA, 1973.

——. *Alaska Trees and Shrubs*, by Leslie A. Viereck and Elbert L. Little. Department of Agriculture Handbook No. 410. Washington, D.C.: USDA, 1972.

——. "Response of Deer to Alternate-strip Clearcutting of Lodgepole Pine and Spruce-Fir Timber in Colorado," by D.C. Wallmo. Note RM-141. Washington, D.C.: USDA, 1969.

——. "Managing for Natural Regeneration," by Hamlin L. Williston and E. Balmer in *Forest Management Bulletin*. Atlanta: USDA, 1974.

U.S. Department of Commerce. *Lumber and Softwood Plywood, U.S.* "Industrial Outlook with 5 Year Projections for 200 Industries." Washington, D.C.: Dept. of Commerce, 1978.

U.S. Department of Commerce. Bureau of the Census. *Current Industrial Reports: Hardwood Plywood*. Washington, D.C.: Bureau of Census, 1976. (issued August 1977).

——. *Current Industrial Reports: Lumber Productions and Mill Stocks*. Washington, D.C.: Bureau of Census, 1976 (issued September 1977).

——. *Current Industrial Reports. Softwood Plywood*. Washington, D.C.: Bureau of Census, 1976 (issued August 1977).

U.S. Department of Commerce. Coast and Geodectic Survey. *Precise Triangulation, Traverse and Leveling in North Carolina*, by Walter D. Sutliffe and Henry G. Avers. Special Pub. No. 101. Washington, D.C.: GPO, 1924.

U.S. Department of the Interior. Fish and Wildlife Service. Division of Management and Enforcement. *Importations of Fish and Wildlife 1969*. Washington, D.C.: Dept. of Interior, 1970.

U.S. Government Printing Office. *Atlas of U.S. Trees*, Vol. I. *Conifers and Important Hardwoods*. Stock No. 001-000-01026. Washington, D.C.: GPO, 1971.

———. *Plants/People/and Environmental Quality*, by G.O. Robinette. Stock No. 024-005-00479-2. Washington, D.C.: GPO, 1972.

National Academy of Sciences. *Vertebrate Pests: Problems and Control.* Series on Principles of Plant and Animal Pest Control, Vol. 5. Washington, D.C.: National Academy of Sciences, 1970.

Reports, Pamphlets, Proceedings

Algvere, Karl. *Outlook for Pulp and Paper Consumption, Production and Trade to 1985.* Second Consultation on World Paper and Paper Demand, Supply and Trade. Rome, Italy: 1971.

Applegate, James E. *Attitudes Toward Deer Hunting in New Jersey: A Second Look.* Bulletin. Wildlife Society, Washington, D.C., 1975.

Anderson, N.W. "Storage and Delivery of Rainfall and Snow Melt Water as Related to Forest Environments" (eds. J.M. Powell and C.F. Nolasco). *1970 Proceedings of the Third Forest Microclimate Symposium*, Seebe, Alberta. Calgary: Canadian Forest Service, 1969.

"Better Logging Cuts Waste." *Multiple-Use Forestry.* Rupert, W.Va.: West-vaco Timberlands Division, Gauley Woodlands, 1978.

Bevins, M.I. and others. *Characteristics of Hunters and Fishermen in Six Northeastern States.* Bulletin 656. Vermont Agricultural Experimental Station. Burlington, Vt.: Univ. of Vermont, 1968.

Bramble, W.C., and English, P.F. "The Forest Grazing Problem Created by Deer in Eastern Forests." *Proceedings of Society of American Foresters.* Washington, D.C., 1948-49.

Conservation Foundation. "National Parks at the Crossroads: Drawing the Line Where Protection Ends and Overuse Begins." Conservation Foundation Newsletter, September 1972.

Davey, Stuart P. "The Role of Wildlife in an Urban Environment." *Proceedings 32nd North American Wildlife and National Resources Conference.* Wildlife Management Institute, Washington, D.C., 1967.

"Energy to Grow." *Westvaco Annual Report.* New York: Westvaco Corporation, 1977.

Findley, W.P.K. "Timber Pests and Diseases." *Pergamon Press Series of Monographs on Furniture and Timber*, 5. Elmsford, N.Y.: Pergamon, 1967.

Forests Industries of Tasmania. Launceston, Tasmania, Australia: Tasmanian Timber Promotion Board, 1977.

"Forest Facts and Figures" (booklet). Washington, D.C.: American Forest Institute. Annual publication.

"Forests of the Future" (pamphlet). New York: Westvaco Corp., 1977.

Fox, Gordon D. Forestry in Developing Countries (preliminary survey). Washington, D.C.: Office of Science and Technology, Agency for International Development, 1972.

Grosenbaugh, L.R. "Optical Dendrometers for Out-of-Reach Diameters: A Conspectus and Some New Theory." *Forest Science Monographs* 4 (1963).

Hegele, T.R. "Landowner's Guide to the North Carolina Forest Development Program." Raleigh, N.C., Agricultural Extension Service, May 1978.

Horvath, Joseph C. "Economic Survey of Wildlife Recreation." Executive Summary. Environmental Research Group. Atlanta: Georgia State University, 1974.

Jackson, L.W.R., Thompson, G.E., and Lund, H.O. *Forest Diseases and Insects of Georgia's Trees*. Georgia Forestry Commission, undated, 40 page pamphlet, p. 8.

Lawrence, K.V.W. "From Mine to Steel 'Taconite'—The Taconite Story" (a brochure). Reprinted from *The Compass* (a publication of the Marine Trade Development, Mobile Sales and Supply Corporation, printed in England), 1968.

McKeever, David B. "Long-term Projections of Demand for Forest Related Outdoor Recreation in the United States." Master's Thesis, Pennsylvania State University, University Park, Pa., 1975.

Poelker, Richard J., and Hartwell, Harry D. "Black Bear of Washington." Biological Bulletin No. 14. Olympia, Wash.: Washington State Game Department, 1973.

Taylor, Samuel, forest management expert, State Forestry Department. Personal communication.

"Timber Harvesting Methods and Equipment of Today and Tomorrow—Needs, Goals and Limitations in New York State." AFRI Misc. Report No. 2, Applied Forest Research Institute. Syracuse, N.Y.: State University College of Forestry at Syracuse Univ., March 1969.

Webster New World Dictionary of the American Language (college edition). Cleveland and New York: The World Publishing Co. Copyright 1958.

Wilderness Withdrawals and Timber Supply. Washington, D.C.: National Forest Products Assoc., January 1978.

Wood, Donald B., and Kennedy, James J. "Noncomsumptive Use of Utah Elk Herd." Outdoor Recreation and Tourism Series. Logan, Utah: Utah State Univ., 1973.

Zasada, Z.A., and Benzie, J.W. "Mechanical Harvesting for Thinning Sawtimber Red Pine." Misc. Report 99. University of Minnesota Forest Service, 1970.

SECONDARY REFERENCE SOURCES

Books

Adams, Ansel, and Newhall, Nancy. *This Is the American Earth*. San Francisco: Sierra Club, 1960.

Alkema, Chester J. *Crafting with Nature's Materials*. New York: Sterling, 1972.

Allen, Gertrude E. *Everyday Trees*. Boston: Houghton Mifflin, 1968.

Allison, Linda. *Reasons for Seasons: The Great Cosmic Megagalactic Trip without Moving from Your Chair*. Boston: Little, Brown, 1975.

Atwood, Ann. *The Kingdom of the Forest*. New York: Scribners, 1972.

Blough, Glenn. *Discovering Plants*. New York: McGraw-Hill, 1966.

——. *Lookout for the Forests*. New York: McGraw-Hill, 1961.

Borland, Hal. *This World of Wonder*. Philadelphia: Lippincott. 1973.

——. *When the Legends Die*. Philadelphia: Lippincott, 1963.

Borten, Helen. *Do You Hear What I Hear?* New York: Abelard, 1950.

——. *Do You See What I See?* New York: Abelard, 1959.

Bromely, W.S., ed. *Pulpwood Production*, 2nd ed. Danville, Ill.: Interstate Printers and Publishers, 1969.

Brown, Vinson. *Reading the Woods: Seeing More in Nature's Familiar Faces.* Harrisburg, Pa.: Stackpole, 1969.

Buck, Margaret W. *In Woods and Field.* Nashville, Tenn.: Abingdon, 1950.

Buff, Mary, and Buff, Conrad. *Big Tree.* New York: Viking, 1946.

Bulla, Clyde R. *A Tree Is a Plant.* New York: Thomas Y. Crowell, 1960.

Busch, Phyllis S. *Once There Was a Tree: The Story of the Tree, A Changing Home for Plants and Animals.* Cleveland: Collins-World, 1972.

Carrick, Carol. *A Clearing in the Forest.* New York: Dial, 1970.

——. *The Tree.* New York: Macmillan, 1971.

Carson, Rachel. *The Sense of Wonder.* New York: Harper & Row, 1965.

Commoner, Barry. *The Closing Circle: Man, Nature and Technology.* New York: Knopf, 1971.

Cooper, Elizabeth K., and Cooper, Padraic. *A Tree Is Something Wonderful.* San Carlos, Calif.: Golden Gate, 1972.

Cosgrove, Margaret. *Wonders of the Tree World*, rev. ed. New York: Dodd, Mead, 1970.

Craven, Margaret. *I Heard the Owl Call My Name.* Garden City, N.Y.: Doubleday, 1973.

Cutler, Katherine. *From Petals to Pine.* New York: Lothrop, 1971.

d'Arbeloff, Natalie. *Designing with Natural Forms.* New York: Watson-Guptill, 1973.

Dana, Samuel T. *A World Geography of Forest Resources.* New York: Ronald Press, 1956.

Darby, Gene. *Finding Out about Plants.* Westchester, Ill.: Benefic, 1974.

Davy, David. *The Buffalo Book: The Full Saga of the American Animal.* Chicago: Swallow, 1973.

DeAngulo, Jaime. *Indian Tales.* New York: Ballantine, 1976.

Dickey, Miriam, and Roth, Charles E. *A Who's Who of Urban America.* Lincoln, Mass.: Massachusetts Audubon Society, 1972.

Dorian, Edith. *Animals That Made U.S. History.* New York: McGraw-Hill, 1964.

Earle, Olive L. *State Trees*, rev. ed. New York: Morrow, 1973.

Ets, Marie H. *In the Forest.* New York: Viking, 1974.

Farb, Peter. *The Face of North America.* New York: Harper & Row, 1964.

Felton, Harold W., ed. *Legends of Paul Bunyan.* New York: Knopf, 1947.

Fenton, Carroll L., and Kitchen, Herminie B. *Plants We Live On: The Story of Grains and Vegetables*, rev. ed. New York: John Day, 1971.

Forest Cover Types of North America (Exclusive of Mexico). Washington, D.C.: Society of American Foresters, 1954.

Franck, Frederick. *The Zen of Seeing.* New York: Knopf, 1973.

Frazier, Beverly. *Nature Crafts and Projects.* Fremont, Calif.: Troubador, 1972.

Fritsch, Albert, and Castleman, Barry I. *Life Style Index.* Washington, D.C.: Center for Science in the Public Interest, 1974.

Gans, Roma. *It's Nesting Time.* New York: Thomas Y. Crowell, 1972.

George, Jean C. *The Hole in the Tree.* New York: Dutton, 1952.

George, John, and George, Jean. *Bubo the Great Horned Owl.* New York: Dutton, 1954.

——. *Masked Prowler: The Story of a Raccoon.* New York: Dutton, 1952.

Gibbons, Euell. *Stalking the Good Life.* New York: McKay, 1971.

Goor, A.Y., and Barney, C.W. *Forest Tree Planting in Arid Zones.* New York: Ronald Press, 1968.

Green, Charlotte H. *Trees of the South*. Chapel Hill, N.C.: University of North Carolina Press, 1939; and New York: Van Rees Press, 1939.

Guilcher, Jean M., and Noailles, R.H. *A Tree Grows Up*. New York: Sterling, 1972.

——. *A Tree Is Born*. New York: Sterling, 1960.

Gussow, Alan. *A Sense of Place. The Artist and the American Land*, 2nd ed. San Francisco: Friends of the Earth, 1974.

Hawkinson, John. *Collect, Print, and Paint from Nature*. Chicago: Whitman, 1953.

Headstrom, Richard. *Adventures with a Hand Lens*. New York: Dover, 1976.

Hutchins, Ross E. *This Is a Leaf*. New York: Dodd, Mead, 1962.

——. *This Is a Tree*. New York: Dodd, Mead, 1964.

Jones, Hettie. *Trees Stand Shining: Poetry of the North American Indians*. New York: Dial, 1971.

Jordan, Helen J. *How A Seed Grows*. New York: Thomas Y. Crowell, 1960.

Joslin, Robert O., and West, Larry. *Colors, Patterns and Textures in Nature*. Chicago: Regnery, 1974.

Klein, Stanley. *A World in a Tree*. Garden City, N.Y.: Doubleday, 1968.

Krauss, Ruth. *The Growing Story*. New York: Harper & Row, 1947.

Kurelek, William. *Lumberjack*. Boston: Houghton Mifflin, 1974.

Liers, Emil E. *Beaver's Story*. New York: Viking, 1958.

McGraw-Hill Book Company. *Technical Composition Standards*. New York: McGraw-Hill, 1966.

Milne, Lorus, and Milne, Margery. *The Phoenix Forest*. New York: Atheneum, 1968.

Murie, Olaus. *Field Guide to Animal Tracks*. Boston: Houghton Mifflin, 1954.

Oppenheim, Joanne. *Have You Seen Trees?* New York: Young Scott, 1967.

Partridge, Arthur D., and Miller Daniel, L. *Major Wood Decays in the Inland Northwest*. Moscow, Idaho: Idaho Research Foundation, 1974.

Platt, Rutherford. *The Great American Forest*. Englewood Cliffs, N.J.: Prentice-Hall, 1971.

Podendorf, Illa. *The True Book of Trees*. Chicago: Childrens Press, 1972.

Pringle, Laurence. *The Only Earth We Have*. New York: Macmillan, 1969.

Roberge, Earl. *Timber Country*. Caldwell, N.J.: Caxton Printers, 1974.

Rounds, Glenn. *Ol' Paul, the Mighty Logger*. New York: Holiday House, 1949.

Russell, Helen R. *The True Book of Buds: Surprise Packages*. Chicago: Childrens Press, 1970.

——. *The Field Trip Guide Series. Winter*, 1972; *Soil*, 1972; *Small Worlds*, 1972; *Water*, 1973. Boston: Little, Brown.

Sancoz, Mari. *The Buffalo Hunters: The Story of the Hide Men*. New York: Hastings House, 1975.

Selsam, Millicent E. *Birth of a Forest*. New York: Harper & Row, 1964.

——. *Hidden Animals*, rev. ed. New York: Harper & Row, 1969.

——. *How To Be a Nature Detective*. New York: Harper & Row, 1966.

——. *Play with Plants*. New York: Morrow, 1949.

——. *Play with Seeds*. New York: Morrow, 1957.

——. *Play with Trees*. New York: Morrow, 1950.

——. *See Through the Forest*. New York: Harper & Row, 1956.

Selsam, Millicent E., and Hunt, Joyce. *A First Look at Leaves*. New York: Walker, 1972.

Showers, Paul. *The Listening Walk*. New York: Thomas Y. Crowell, 1961.

Shuttlesworth, Dorothy. *Animal Camouflage*. Garden City, N.Y.: Doubleday, 1966.

——. *Natural Partnerships*. Garden City, N.Y.: Doubleday, 1969.

Silverberg, Robert. *Vanishing Giants: The Story of the Sequoias*. New York: Simon & Schuster, 1969.

Stokes, Jack. *Let's Be Nature's Friend!* New York: McKay, 1976.

Strache, Wolf. *Forms and Patterns in Nature*. New York: Pantheon, 1973.

Tanner, Thomas R. *Ecology, Environment and Education*. Lincoln, Neb.: Professional Educators Publications, 1974.

Taylor, Benjamin D. *Design Lessons from Nature*. New York: Watson-Guptill, 1974.

Trefethen, James B. *The American Landscape: 1776-1976, Two Centuries of Change*. Washington, D.C.: Wildlife Management Institute, 1976.

Tresselt, Alvin. *The Beaver Pond*. New York: Lothrop, 1970.

Udry, Janice M. *A Tree Is Nice*. New York: Harper & Row, 1956.

Vevers, Gwyne. *Birds and Their Nests*. New York: McGraw-Hill, 1973.

Wahlenberg, W.G. *Loblolly Pine*. Durham, N.C.: Duke University, 1960.

Webber, Irma. *Bits That Grow Big: Where Plants Come From*. New York: Young Scott, 1949.

——. *Thanks to Trees: The Story of Their Use and Conservation*. New York: Young Scott, 1957.

Wong, Herbert H., and Vessel, Matthew F. *Our Tree*. Reading, Mass.: Addison-Wesley, 1969.

Yepsen, Robert B., Jr. *Trees for the Yard, Orchard and Woodlot*. Emmaus, Pa.: Rodale, 1976.

Zim, Herbert S. *What's Inside of Plants*. New York: Morrow, 1952.

Periodicals

Beardsley, Wendell G., and Wagar, J.A. "Vegetation Management on a Forested Recreation Site." *Journal of Forestry* 69 (October 1971): 729-731.

Cobb, Fields W., Jr., and Stark, R.W. "Decline and Mortality of Smog-Injured Ponderosa Pine." *Journal of Forestry* 68 (1970): 147-49.

Crebbin, Peter A. "Tree Length Operation in Lodgepole Pine." *Loggers Handbook* 29 (1969): 21-23, 44.

Davis, M.H. "Maintaining an Effective Organization to Control the Occasional Large Fire." *Journal of Forestry* 52 (1954): 750-55.

Dell, John D., and Green, Lisle R. "Slash Treatment in the Douglas-fir Region—Trends in the Pacific Northwest." *Journal of Forestry* 66 (1968): 610-14.

De Wyngaert, Laura. "Art Interprets Nature." *Arts and Activities* 69 (April 1971): 13-16.

Grinstead, Robert R. "The New Resource." *Environment* 12 (December 1970): 2-17.

Hannon, Bruce M. "Bottles, Cans, Energy." *Environment* 12 (March 1972): 11-21.

Harmon, Dudley. "Will New England Take a Change?" *American Forests* 45 (1939): 180-81, 228.

Headley, Roy. "Who Starts These Fires?" *American Forests* 45 (1939): 191-93.

Isaacs, Jon. "Environmental Mythology." *Environmental Education Report* 2 (November 1974): 3-5.

Jackson, M.T., and Petty, R.O. "A Simple Optical Device for Measuring Vertical Projection of Tree Crowns." *Forest Science* 19(1973): 60-62.

McCulley, R.D. "The Case for Even-aged Management of Southern Pine." *Journal of Forestry* 51 (1953): 88-90.

McDonald, W.J. "Fire under the Midnight Sun." *American Forests* 45 (1939): 168-69.

McNary, Charles L. "Forest Fires—Challenge to Federal Leadership." *American Forests* 45 (1939): 199.

Mcsavage, Clement. "Measuring Bark Thickness." *Journal of Forestry* 67 (1969): 40-41.

Minckler, L. "Ecological Bookkeeping." *American Forests* 79 (August 1973): 20-23.

Mines, Samuel. "Again and Again and Again and . . . A Report on Recycling." *Ecology Today* 1 (March 1971): 23-25.

Mobley, Hugh E. "Fire: Its Impact on the Environment." *Journal of Forestry* 22 (1974): 414-17.

Murphy, E.W. "California Pays the Red Piper." *American Forests.* 45 (1939): 202-04.

Siecke, E.O. "Getting Results by Law Enforcement." *American Forests* 45 (1939): 212-13.

Silcox, F.A. "Men against the Flames." *American Forests* 45 (1939): 194-98.

Smithsonian Institute. "Scenes . . . from Which the Hand of Nature Has Never Been Lifted." *Smithsonian* 3 (1972): 34-41.

Sprague, Charles A. "What Forest Fire Control Means to the Northwest." *American Forests* 45 (1939): 165-67.

Swingler, W.S. "Keeping Forest Insects in Their Place." *American Forests* 65 (1959): 28-45.

Tresselt, Alvin. "The Dead Tree." *Parents Magazine* (1972).

Van Naverbeke, David F., and Cook, David I. "Green Mufflers." *American Forests* 78 (November 1972): 28-31.

Watt, Kenneth F. "Man's Efficient Rush toward Deadly Dullness." *Natural History* 81 (February 1972): 74-77.

Westveld, R.H. "A Challenge for the Wood Products Industries." *Journal of Forestry* 66 (1968): 471-474.

Federal and State Government Publications

Arizona Department of Transportation. "Indian Basketmaking." *Arizona Highways* 51 (July 1975).

United Nations. *Tropical Silviculture*, by I.T. Haig, M.A. Huberman, and U. Aung. Din. Rome, Italy: Food and Agriculture Organization of the United Nations, 1958.

U.S. Department of Agriculture. *Nursery Diseases of Southern Pines*, by A.A. Foster. Forest Pest Leaflet No. 32. Washington, D.C.: USDA, 1959.

——. *Insect Enemies of Western Forests*, by F.P. Keen. Washington, D.C.: USDA, 1952.

——. "Windbreaks and Shelterbelts," in *Trees* by Joseph H. Stoeckler and Ross A. Williams. Washington, D.C.: USDA, 1949.

——. *Timber Resources for America's Future*, Forest Service Report No. 14. Washington, D.C.: USDA, 1958.

——. *Natural Regeneration of Loblolly Pine in the South Atlantic Coastal Plain*, by Karl Wenger and K.B. Trousdell. Washington, D.C.: USDA, 1958.

U.S. Department of Agriculture. Forest Service. *The National Fire-Danger Rating System.* Research Paper RM-84 Fort Collins, Colo.: USDA, 1974.

——. *Natural Regeneration of White and Red Fir: Influence of Several Factors,* by Donald T. Gordon. Research Paper PSW-58. Washington, D.C.: USDA, 1970.

——. *Checklist of Native and Naturalized Trees of the United States,* by E.L. Little. Agriculture Handbook No. 41. Washington, D.C.: USDA, 1953.

——. *Northeastern Loggers Handbook,* by Fred C. Simmons. Agriculture Handbook No. 6. Washington, D.C.: USDA, 1951.

——. Table on Insects, Trees Affected, Nature of Damage and Control. Research Triangle Park, N.C.: USDA Forestry Science Laboratory, 1979.

U.S. Department of Commerce. *Pulp, Paper and Board and Converted Products.* U.S. Industrial Outlook with 5 Year Projections for 200 Industries. Washington, D.C.: Dept. of Commerce, 1978.

U.S. Department of Commerce. Bureau of the Census. *Statistical Abstract of the U.S. National Data Book and Guide to Sources.* Washington, D.C.: Dept. of Commerce, 1977.

U.S. Department of the Interior. "Press Release on Lands in Alaska." Dept. of the Interior, 1973.

U.S. Department of Labor. Bureau of Labor Statistics. *Occupational Outlook Handbook,* 1978–79 ed. Bulletin No. 1955. Washington, D.C.: Dept. of Labor, 1978.

Reports, Pamphlets, Proceedings

"Attempt to Stop Water Fowl Hunting Stalled." News Release. Wildlife Management Institute, Washington, D.C., November 1974.

Conservation Directory. National Wildlife Federation, Washington, D.C., 1977.

"Forests and Trees of the U.S." (a map), 1971 ed. American Forest Institute, Washington, D.C.

Herendeen, R., and Selbald, Anthony V. *The Dollar, Energy and Employment Impacts of Certain Consumer Options.* No. 97. Center for Advanced Computation University of Illinois, Urbana, Ill. 1974.

Hirt, Ray R. "Blister Rust, A Serious Disease of White Pine." New York State College of Forestry, Syracuse, N.Y., 1933.

National Survey of State Fish and Wildlife Funding. Wildlife Management Institute, Washington, D.C., 1975.

Shaw, William A. *Meanings of Wildlife for Americans: Contemporary Attitudes and Social Trends.* 39th North American Wildlife and Natural Resources Conference. Wildlife Management Institute, Washington, D.C., 1974.

Steen, Harold K. *The U.S. Forest Service—A History.* Seattle, Wash.: University of Washington Press, 1977.

Index